HUNGRY

Grace Dent

HUNGRY

A story of growing up
and wanting more

MUDLARK

Mudlark
An imprint of HarperCollins*Publishers*
1 London Bridge Street
London SE1 9GF

www.harpercollins.co.uk

First published by Mudlark 2020
This paperback edition published 2021

3 5 7 9 10 8 6 4 2

© Grace Dent 2020

Grace Dent asserts the moral right to be
identified as the author of this work

A catalogue record of this book is
available from the British Library

ISBN 978-0-00-833318-8

Printed and Bound in the UK using 100% Renewable Electricity at
CPI Group (UK) Ltd

MIX
Paper from
responsible sources
FSC
www.fsc.org
FSC™ C007454

This book is produced from independently certified FSC™ paper
to ensure responsible forest management.

For more information visit: www.harpercollins.co.uk/green

For David Dent.
The funniest person I know.

Contents

This is a sort of memoir.

It's about my memories.

Other people's memories of how my life happened may differ.

Names have been changed in order to give privacy to people who never imagined their secrets would end up in a book published by HarperCollins.

Some places, events, dates and times have also been changed for that reason.

The past is a foreign country; they eat chips differently there.

Grace Dent, 2020

'When I was a little lass, the world was half a dozen streets, an' a bit o' waste land, an' the rest was all talk.'

Ena Sharples, *Coronation Street*, 1965

CHAPTER 1

Sketty

Carlisle, 2017

'Where would you say Carlisle is, George?'

I shift uncomfortably in my seat.

'Where's Carlisle?' the nurse repeats.

My dad does not answer.

'Have you heard of it?'

I look at my phone, merely to self-soothe.

Instead, an email from a *Guardian* editor arrives, begging for the incredibly late 800-word restaurant column that I had promised to write on the 10.03 out of Euston. I did not write the piece. Instead, I placed my face against the cold window and drifted off, letting Milton Keynes become Wigan North Western become Shap become home.

'Can you have a guess?' she says. He looks at her and says nothing. His silence wounds me.

The nurse marks something down in her notes.

I look at her and maintain my gaze. She believes me, doesn't she? She looks away, sharply.

Carlisle, summer 1980

My dad is making sketty for our tea. And I am helping, because I'm seven years old and nothing goes on in this house that I don't have my nose in.

Any rustlings of supermarket carrier bags, any raised voices, any arrival at the front door of 21 Harold Street, I'll know about them. Tonight my dad's in charge, as my mother is out doing the job that she doesn't like mentioned. My dad's childcare regime, like that of most Seventies dads, is a rudimentary affair. As long as we've had food, we're allowed to 'play out' until it's dark. Sometimes later. We roam free over two square miles of back-to-back terraced streets and fields. We're warned to mind the busier roads. Me, my little brother David and the eleven or so kids from along Harold Street 'play out' for hours and hours, chucking tennis balls at the sides of the houses and hurtling ourselves on roller skates down the cement slope from the nearby Bishop Goodwin C of E Primary School car park. Or we'll break off in splinter groups into different kids' bedrooms. I'm often found loitering around Tracey Scaleby's house at Number 17, sending Sindy dolls on a sexy caravan holiday with her brother Scott's Action Men, a burly gang with eagle eyes and clasping hands. On Sundays we go to the Currock Villa Youth Club and dance in long formation lines to 'Freedom' by Wham!, throwing our arms in the air to 'once, twice, forever', and then we'll play dodge-the-local-shady-grown-up-helper-who-wants-to-wrestle-you-for-a-little-bit-too-long.

On warmer nights we'll take the bags of misshapen mint Viscounts our aunties buy us from the factory shop inside Carr's biscuit factory down to the abandoned allotments near the West Coast mainline railway track, which takes you the 317 miles into Euston, London – a terrible dirty place where everyone is unfriendly. It's not like here. If you got attacked in the street in London, no one would help you. They'd pretend not to see. Not like in Carlisle where folk would shout and scream at bad people and think it was wrong.

We take our biscuits down to where the gypsies keep their horses and feed the tamer ones bread crusts from our mams' bread bins. Or we'll play houses or make grass cuttings into the boundaries of princess castles. We'll hurtle through hedges playing Japs and Commanders. We'll sit in our favourite den inside an enormous overgrown bush, sharing bottles of Barr's Scotch Cola and leafing curiously through tattered copies of *Fiesta*, gawping at women in no knickers holding their knees apart. Sometimes we'll roam beyond our boundary of Currock, wantonly searching out the dens that belong to rival gangs of kids from nearby Carlisle districts like Upperby, Harraby or Botcherby. We howl with glee as we stomp all over their leafy hideouts.

But I am equally happy when I'm indoors just kicking about with my dad, and tonight we're making sketty – the more complex of his two-recipe artillery. His other stock standard is baked beans on fried bread. At a push he could open a tin of corned beef. Sometimes – and this is the very best possible turn of events – we'll get a bag of Salt 'n' Shake crisps and fifty pence to buy us all chocolate at Cellar Five, the off-licence at the end of Harold Street. My little brother David likes a Curly Wurly and my dad, always, a bar of Cadbury's Fruit & Nut. My big brother Bob doesn't stay in with us anymore. He lives at Gran's house sometimes. Now seventeen, he comes and he goes, always with hair that antagonises my mother – too long, too short, too dyed, too spikey; the neighbours must be having a field day – often off out to one of the many pubs in Carlisle that serve the underage unblinkingly.

My dad sits in his chair and skims his thumbnail through the foil on his chocolate. I will never see Cadbury's purple without thinking of my father. Cadbury's purple is love. Cadbury's purple is me and him toddling slowly back from the NAAFI shop before he left the forces. My first memories of Dad are him in his REME (Royal Electrical and Mechanical Engineers) uniform in 1976. Me holding one finger of his big hand, examining the puddles, dawdling; both of us laughing together. Me carrying a bag of Cadbury's Buttons with a nursery rhyme of 'Little Jack Horner' on the side. Cadbury's purple is two identical Dairy Milk Easter eggs from Gran. One for me, one for David, perched on the top shelf of the living-room dresser. We are forbidden to touch them before Good Friday when Jesus gets on his cross. The waiting is agony. Cadbury's means being sent down the 'offy'. That said, I'm also partial to a Rowntree's Lion Bar, as it lasts longer than other chocolate. It is the best thing ever when David wolfs down his Curly Wurly in two minutes and I'm still sat watching *World in Action*, languishing through at least two more inches of knobbly chocolate heaven.

Dad lets me peel an onion. He lets me take a knife with a serrated edge and begin to chop it up on our glass chopping board. The knife isn't that sharp. None of the knives in our house are sharp. The onion makes my eyes weep, but I am not put off as I've watched a lovely lady called Delia who cooks every Saturday on Noel Edmonds' *Multi-coloured Swap Shop* and she says that the onion tears are normal.

Me and Dad locate one of our cheap, stained frying pans and Dad puts it on the most reliable electric ring and adds a glug of Spry Crisp 'n Dry. We add the onion and Dad smooshes it around in the warming oil with a wooden fish slice as it gently softens.

My dad's large blue inky tattoo scrawled across the hazelnut-brown skin on his lower right arm will never not be fascinating. Nor will his refusal to answer questions about it.

'What is it?' I say.

'Oh, it's a daft thing I did in the army,' he mumbles.

'Is it a picture?' I say. 'A lion? Is that bit a heart? It looks like a heart.'

'No, it's just a thing,' he says, moving things on.

'Is that a word?' I say, tracing the smudged letters under the blurred picture. 'V? E?'

He has put the spatula in my hand. Now I am smooshing the onion.

'Mind what yer doin'. Yer don't wannalerritburn,' he says.

'I'm not lerrin' it burn,' I say, my accent already speckled with his Merseyside tones.

My father was born on the Scotland Road in Liverpool. He is known to all his old ex-army crowd, and in his civilian role now with the RAF, as simply 'Scouse'. Dad is there in some of the ways I sound my words. In the way I laugh and the way I have begun to make other people laugh. Liverpool genes are like a rogue pair of red knickers in the washing machine with your whites. They leave a trace.

Softening an onion will be a lesson that lasts a lifetime. It will be the genesis of shepherd's pie, frittata and a thousand restorative soups, stews and curries. Decades later, I will attempt to teach highly intelligent, otherwise practical friends to cook and realise that the fine art of onion softening is almost unteachable. It is a deeply mindful act that needs to be carried out absent-mindedly.

Now into the pan we tip a pound of raw beef mince bought from the local Co-op butcher's counter. It stinks something awful at first as I mash it about, like flesh, like something wrong, but as it browns and meets the onion it becomes marginally less disgusting. My childhood – in fact, almost *all* British childhoods in the 1970s and 80s – contains a lot of mince. Mince in a pie, made on a plate at my gran's house in a kitchen that always smelled vaguely but rather deliciously of gas. Mince in bread-crumbed Findus Crispy Pancakes with McCain oven chips after swimming lessons. Mince *inside* a ball of mashed potato, battered, from Donny's Chip Shop on the Five Road Ends in Currock.

Sometimes when my dad gets home from work he gets a piece of steak. Maybe now and then a piece of liver with fried onions, although offal is generally balked at in our house. My mam and dad grew up through the 1940s and 50s when tripe and tongue were delivered to your front door by mobile van. It lurked, unrefrigerated, hairy, veiny, in the pantry for days. They lived through mysterious faggots and dripping smeared on toast. They lived through guts, stomach linings and offcuts being the only options. By the time I appeared in the 1970s, a nice sterile tin of Fray Bentos Chicken Pie felt to them like progress. Or a shiny tin of Spam, so cheap and so easy to cut. Sirloin steak, if you were lucky enough to afford it, was fried 'well done'. Only 'that French lot' ate it with blood. Steak, to us, was the epitome of fine eating. A symbol of eating like a king, living like rich people do. Today, the moneyed boho foodie crowd revel in eating the gnarliest, most disgusting parts of any animal. The brains. The tendons. The ears. The hooves. 'Oh, the pig's tail is the most delicious part, Grace. Just flash-fry them with Szechuan peppercorns and some Madeira wine and eat them with your fingers. Try them with a good New World Burgundy!' But it will be at least 2018 before I see one of my Dent family order something as outré as a slow-cooked beef cheek. Why put yourself through that when something as openly delicious as a gammon steak with a fried egg is on offer?

* * *

I push the browned mince around the pan. It is time for its glamorous transformation into bolognaise. But I won't know this word for several more years; I'll just carry on calling it sketty. This is dad's Scouse way of saying 'spaghetti'. His recipe is Spag Bol à la Skelmersdale and the magic ingredient is a tin of Campbell's Condensed Cream of Tomato Soup. It flops out of its tin in a vivid orange, coagulated, tube-shaped lump. Condensed soup was how we did 'Italian' in Currock. I did not see a bulb of garlic until the mid-Eighties and that was round the neck of someone in a beret in *'Allo 'Allo*, to illustrate that they were truly French. It will be at least the late-Nineties when I accept the wild nonsense that celery, carrots, milk and bay leaves should form a delicate *sofritto* base to Italian sauces or stews. On the other hand, I will always think that hurling a small can of Heinz Baked Beans into a spag bol is no disaster if you need to make it stretch further. As for seasoning, my dad's cooking only ever had nods towards it. 'Salt,' Dad says, nudging the big barrel over to me. I fling two handfuls in. Salt is brilliant. Salt makes everything nicer. Then, a liberal shake of Saxa ground white pepper from a white plastic canister – grey, powdery and liable to fly up my dad's big nose and make him sneeze.

Our road, Harold Street, is a row of terraced houses in the most northern part of North-West England, eight miles from the border of Scotland, close to where Hadrian built his wall. I was born in Aldershot, where we lived on the army base. We moved to Carlisle soon after, back to my mother's hometown, first living in a council house on the outskirts, before my parents bought their first home. Our house sits in the centre of the row. It is newly pebble-dashed, with a front door that opens straight into the living room. Like every dad along Harold Street, all my dad wants is a quiet life, the pinnacle of which would be to read his paper every night. Reading the newspaper is one of Dad's only interests. His others are squirting WD-40 at squeaky things and watching telly in his armchair uninterrupted. But for George, this peace is constantly marred by the endless flinging open of the front door, followed by five or more children running past, heading for the muddy back lane behind our terrace. This is a time before 'playdates' and long before scheduled fun. The kids along Harold Street live largely to their own schedule. We are always in and out and in again at 21 Harold Street, shouting and sobbing and sometimes carrying a kitten. We are bouncing past on pogo sticks and begging to make Rice Krispie cakes for the *Blue Peter* bring-and-buy sale, and always, always leaving the door wide open and makin a drrraughhht.

Dad stands at the stove sliding an entire packet of spaghetti out of its long plastic covering and snapping it in half to fit it into a pan of cold water. The pan will take at least half an hour to come to the boil on our temperamental stove, but this will give me time to find David. At half past six, along Harold Street the air will be peppered by a dozen front doors opening and the yelling of names.

'Tracccccccey?

'Gerrard?'

'Kevin?'

'Daaaaaaaavid, yer tea's ready, gerrrrrinside!'

Dave appears, pulling his Raleigh Tomahawk through the living room like he's been told not to twenty times.

Me, Dave and Dad eat the sketty from bowls on our laps using old copies of the *Evening News* to stop our knees getting hot. We watch the end of the news show *Nationwide* or *Play Your Cards Right*, or *The Krypton Factor*, where brave contenders in Bri-Nylon tracksuits puff and pant around an army assault course. Dad's sketty is always, always delicious. Comforting, sweet and gloriously stodgy, because Dad boiled the pasta for at least thirty to forty minutes too long.

I eat it without thinking about calories or portion size. I am hungry and I devour it freely and take second helpings if there's any left, filling my belly without the smallest trace of guilt.

I am not a cuddly child. I am a slightly Machiavellian one who hates being sent off to bed, and I can always stay up later if I wheedle my way under my dad's musky armpit and stay very quiet. Now invisible, I keep my trap shut, lapping up *The Professionals*. Or, very best of all, *The Kenny Everett Video Show* with my absolute hero, Cleo Rocos. Cleo is an amazingly funny lady with big messy hair and lipstick and smudged eye make-up, who often only wears her knickers and sexy stockings, and her friend is a man called Kenny who sometimes pretends to be a punk. It is naughty and silly and rude and I am not meant to be watching it, which makes it all the more delicious. At the beginning every week, the Thames Television ident flashes up with a loud triumphant jingle. It is terrifying and exhilarating all at once. It's a bright-blue skyline with St Paul's Cathedral, Big Ben and the Post Office Tower reflected in the bright-blue River Thames. In London, Cleo and Kenny hang out all day long and have fun together and I want to be there too. But London is a very, very long way away from Carlisle. It is the other side of the world.

At some point, my mam will return from her job cleaning the betting shop, carrying a tattered copy of the *Sun* with all the racing fixtures and results filleted out of the back. I snap it up and sit reading the sexy problem page and puzzling over the vital statistics of the Page Three stunnas.

'Nikki is 36-24-36! She'd love to work in a zoo one day … but for now she's just making you fellas growl with pleasure!' These measurements are destined to be seared on my brain forever as I stare down sadly at a tape measure a hundred times through my life.

My mother, incidentally, would strenuously deny that I was allowed to stay up past 10 p.m., aged seven years old, reading the *Sun* problem page. My mother's capacity for denial and revisionism would make Chairman Mao blush. She still claims she did not refuse to buy one of my infant school photos because it was taken on a day when I had a sty on my right eye and she'd cut my fringe wonky, so I looked like a small Hunchback of Notre Dame. 'Well, we're not gonna put that thing on the shelf, are we?' she hooted, stuffing the photos all back in the envelope. I would say that I remember this specifically happening. My mother would say that I have an overactive imagination and have always made things up. We have been having a variation of this argument roughly three times a week since at least 1978.

Inevitably, something smutty will occur on the telly: a pair of tits, a swear word, something that reminds Mam we're past the watershed and she'll look up from her sewing and say, 'That child should be in bed!'

My dad will wrap his arm around me, cuddle me into his armpit and say, 'Oh, give her five more minutes here ... she's my only little girl ...'

My mother will roll her eyes and say, 'You're as thick as bloody thieves, you two.'

And he'll say, 'Oh, she's my only little girl.'

And at this point in time, I have no reason not to believe him.

November 1980

'Six spoons of it. That's what we agreed,' my mother snaps.

'I've had six,' I lie.

'You've had three,' she says.

I am sitting on our brown squeaky leather sofa, peering mournfully into a bowl of tepid Ready Brek. My mother, also called Grace, is scribbling on the back of the gas bill with a BIC biro. She's doing some rough maths. She is planning some home improvements. It is not good enough that we merely own a home now. She must make it better. These types of doodlings will provide a constant source of peril during my formative years. They mean we will spend at least the next three months in a thin layer of cement dust while walls are being knocked through and other ones built.

'If I put the door there,' she says, 'then it'll stop the draughts and yer dad might stop being a mard-arse,' she says.

It's eight o'clock in the morning, but Mam is already brimming with ideas about 'partition walls' and 'opaque glass'. That is, I learn, glass you can but can't see though, which sounds weird but at the same time very classy.

The bleak lukewarm oatmeal mulch in my bowl has grown a skin.

Mam stops doodling and stares at me. Her mid-length Diana Dors blonde hair spills down over her purple Marshall Ward-catalogue dressing gown.

'Gerritdownya,' she says, pointing at the Ready Brek. 'A car cannot run without petrol.'

'Ammnot a car,' I argue. 'Noteatingit.'

'You bloody are,' she says.

Mam has been promised by a new TV campaign for Ready Brek – running in every ad break – that this porridgey slop in an orange box will be the solution to one of her other biggest problems. That neither of her infant-school-age children will touch breakfast. This makes her a very lacking mother indeed.

'*Breakfast is the most important meal of the day,*' she's been hectored for decades – by her own mother, by the government and by her teachers. It is her sole responsibility to administer it. Except that morning after morning, as Terry Wogan pipes 'Forever and Ever' by Demis Roussos across the ether on BBC Radio 2, we have rejected all of her options.

Eggs were her first try; she poached them and served them on toasted Mothers Pride. But her whites went all stringy and the toast turned soggy, as she didn't drain them properly. She then moved on to dippy soft-boiled eggs with soldiers, which we turned our noses up at. The good thing about the egg stage was that at Bishop Goodwin Infant School we were collecting the shells to make a large mural of Jesus entering Jerusalem on a donkey. It was a religious school; we found bold new ways every term to praise the lord.

After eggs, Mam tried Weetabix with warm milk, which we complained was both too sludgy, too soggy *and* too dusty all at once. She tried us with toast and orange marmalade, but the bitter slugs of rind caused hysteria. She tried us on Scott's Porage Oats – very grown-up this felt – and let us add our own heaped teaspoons of Silver Spoon sugar.

But that was ruined by her admitting that our eccentric great-uncle, John, in the days before refrigerators, used to make his porridge once a week, pour it into a kitchen drawer to set, then cut a slice out of the coagulated lump each morning. By Friday, Uncle John's breakfast would inevitably contain a beetle or two, she admitted.

Well, that was it for us with the oats. Game over.

Eventually Mam caved in and splashed out on the Kellogg's Variety pack of mini-cereals that David and I had become utterly fixated on after Karen Steeple's mam down the street got some to take with them on their caravan holiday in Filey.

They were exactly the same as big packets of cereal … but smaller.

Our tiny minds were blown.

'Can we have the mini-cereals, Mam? Can we?'

Of course, once we'd got them, ripped open the cellophane, rejected the Bran Flakes and remembered we didn't much care for Rice Krispies anyway, she was back to square one.

And now it's November and there's snow on the ground and she's been promised that Ready Brek is 'central heating for kids' and it'll send me to school with a glowing aura around me. But I'm not having it.

'Mam, it's just the same stuff as the porridge, but slimier!' I cry.

'Oh, shut up,' she says.

Winter's arrival also means stiff north-westerly winds blasting the back of Dad's head continuously as me and my brother fling open the front door, coming and going into the street to play. And then he 'starts whining', she says, or 'being narky'. My parents, although I do not know this at the time, have been married precisely eight years. They made that decision in haste and spent the Eighties repenting at leisure.

But, on one front at least, things were about to improve.

Because we were getting a vestibule.

'A vestibule?' I repeat.

This all sounds very grand.

Mam shows me her drawings.

It sounds continental and by default insanely glamorous. Like something JR's house would have in *Dallas*.

It's like nothing anyone else has along Harold Street and is most probably the beginnings of my working-class delusions of grandeur.

'We'll take a bit off the living room,' Mam says, 'so when you come in the front door … there will be a little space … then another door!'

'Like another little room inside the room?' I say.

'Yes … and we can have coat pegs in there,' she says. 'And a little table to put letters on. And maybe a shelf for our books …'

Her voice trails off.

The only books we have are a *News of the World* part-work on serial killers and a copy of *The Thorn Birds*.

'OK, maybe we could put the phone in there,' she says brightly. 'And the phone book. Anyway, no more draughts.'

I stare at her and then back at the Ready Brek. I've eaten five whole teaspoons of the stuff and I seem to have more of the evil sludge than when I set off.

Seven days later, with a swiftness that accompanied many of my mother's good ideas, work began. Frank the carpenter arrived with a spirit level under his arm and a pencil crammed behind his filthy left ear.

He needed half the money up front for the wood, panes and the paint, and he'd have the job done between Tuesday and Friday as long as he could work until after midnight.

'Dad, do *you* want a vestibule?' I asked, as a terrific banging and clattering began and we all cowered in the kitchen, covered in dust.

'Well, your mother does,' Dad said. 'She's full of these good ideas.'

News of the vestibule spread quickly along Harold Street. The neighbours were transfixed. It must have felt a lot like when Pope Julius II got artists in to do the Sistine Chapel. Except our vestibule was being hammered up by a man called Frank, who turned up every night after six o'clock, as he was being spied on by the dole office. Almost everyone who did odd jobs on Harold Street during this time was 'signed off on the permanent sick' from Cavaghan & Gray pie factory with bad backs.

'He could not move until that day, your honour,' local lawyer Geoff Clapp would say, defending another of my mother's friends caught skipping out of a cul-de-sac in Morton Park carrying a twelve-foot stepladder and fifteen litres of Crown Marigold Emulsion, despite a debilitating spinal condition.

In my mother's mind, family bliss was only ever one more home improvement away. First came the pebble-dashing.

'George, the stones add an extra layer of warmth to the house! Our gas bills will be right down,' she informed my dad, as two listless skinheads on a Youth Training Scheme hurled around handfuls of shilly. 'It *adds value* if we ever sell!' she added. Before that, she added a spare toilet just off the kitchen to stop the arguments when anyone spent too long in the upstairs one. She did this by paying someone to hammer up MDF boards roughly two feet south of the chip pan. This was great as you could wee and still mind your fish fingers. The vestibule, however, was her most ambitious project to date – and she had her naysayers, like Stella at Number 3, who said it would make our front room poky, but things like that don't derail a good woman like my mam.

I learned tenacity from her. I learned from the best.

When I was a little girl, my mother felt like a preternatural force. She was five foot ten with golden hair and pale-blue eyes. She had been married once before she met my dad. I didn't know many facts about this, but I thought it was very exciting. Mam laughed a lot but was frightening as hell when angry. She would threaten to kill us often. Strangle us. She could, if the mood took her, move large items of furniture all on her own.

It made no sense, us all facing that way, she'd say, when we came home from school at lunch to find the couch and TV somewhere else.

In a time before health and safety, she would pull up outside Bishop Goodwin Juniors on netball-match day, cram nine girls in blue bibs into her Austin Princess and ferry them across town, no seatbelts, faces squashed against the windows, off to play Kingmoor Primary.

She was a woman who just got things done.

So within days, when you opened the front door to 21 Harold Street, you stepped into a brilliant-white, gloss-painted, three-foot-by-three porch.

But *please*, this was not a porch.

This was a vestibule.

'We can hang out in my vestibule,' I'd say airily as rain began to beat onto Harold Street's flagstones, ruining our evening of chewing Hubba Bubba and swinging around a lamppost. Excitedly, we would tumble into the space. This was my own mini youth club. Obviously, this meant my father was now reading his *Carlisle Evening News* four feet away from five kids doing a dance routine to 'September' by Earth, Wind & Fire with only partition wood separating us.

But, importantly, there was no longer a draught on his back, and this made him happier. And for a small moment in history, we had the poshest house along Harold Street, which made my mam happier too.

'So, the vestibule,' she said, weeks later as I sat before school eating a breakfast she had recently chanced upon that I'd begun to secretly enjoy – Shippam's Sardine & Tomato Paste on toast with real butter. My mother had marked this as 'something our Grace likes' and was now making noises about something horrific called Bloater Paste.

'Did I do the right thing, then?' she said, pointing to the opaque glass and fresh paintwork.

'Yer, it's smart as owt. I love it,' I told her.

Over the last few years, as I've struggled to make sense of the present, I've thought about that living room in Harold Street: me, David, Mam, Dad, sometimes my big brother Bob appearing temporarily from the terrific din of Bowie, Japan and The

Specials that always blared from his room when he was around. I've thought about nights when we'd sit around watching *Name That Tune* with Lionel Blair, eating bowls of butterscotch Angel Delight and Neapolitan ice cream and passing round the big red tin of Rover Assorted Biscuits, fighting over the pink wafers until only the crap ones were left. I've thought about us all in the living room, snug as bugs because the vestibule cut out the draughts, and always chattering and fighting and telling each other to bloody shut up as this is the only programme they want to watch and now everyone is blabbing on. I've thought about how there's a weird happiness in the rhythms of a cat coughing up hairballs as five people bicker over who last had the *News of the World* TV supplement, until someone stands up to go to the loo and gets lumped with the chore of doing four rounds of toast.

I would give anything to go back there for just one normal evening. I was loved and I was never hungry, and for a small girl from Currock, that was as good as things got.

Carlisle, 1982

'Warm up the teapot,' says Brown Owl, 'by pouring a little hot water in and swirling it around!'

I'm doing my Hostess Brownie badge; that's the one where you plop a teabag in a pot and arrange some Custard Creams on a plate before serving them to Brown Owl's husband, Trevor, who plays the part of 'an important man who you're on your best behaviour for'. Trevor takes a biscuit and pretends to ignore my hands shaking as I pour his drink.

Aged eight, there is much to cherish about being part of the eighteenth Carlisle Methodist Church Brownie Pack. The Brownies attempted to teach me discipline, forward planning, a sense of duty and, best of all, it gave me my first formal lessons in how to cook and entertain. Plus, there was a cool brown tunic pulled in at the waist with a brown buckled belt and a yellow cravat tie with a Velcro tie strip. I especially loved the shiny silver shamrock Brownie badge that we got after enrolment. This ceremony involved pirouetting around a large rusting metal 'toadstool' splodged with red and green paint, unlocked from the cleaner's cupboard for this most grand of occasions. Dad came to my enrolment and watched from the sidelines, sitting on a stiff-back chair. He didn't fall asleep once. Dad was rarely trusted to take me or my little brother anywhere outside the house after he fell asleep in Carlisle Odeon Cinema during a trip to see *The Boys in Blue* with Cannon & Ball. He only woke up when the usher pinched him and asked if those were his kids in the foyer. My dad looked dead proud when Brown Owl gave me my badge, and I think he was glad he came; even if his head was lolling about sleepily during our mid-ceremony performance, when eighteen girls sang 'Alice the Camel' in a three-part round.

My second badge was House Orderly: a two-week crash course on shopping-list crafting, bed-making and dust vigilance. On reflection, this primed millions of little girls across

Britain for a life, someday soon, as some bloke's skivvy, but
at this point trying to make an imaginary fiver stretch to feed
a family for a week seemed like a terrific game. Then on to
my Cookery badge. For this, Trevor got half a grapefruit, a
scrambled egg on toast and a serviette folded into a triangle.
The 1980s Brownie ethos, unlike today, contained no mention
of us girls striving towards a career or a vocation. There were
no balm-like words on body image or self-belief. We had been
put on earth to be really, really helpful. The highlight of each
Thursday-night meeting was when we separated into our
three sub-sets – the Pixies, the Elves and the Gnomes – and
sang our little theme tunes: 'Here we come, the jolly Pixies,
helping others with their fixes!' Or 'Here we are, the happy
Elves, we think of others, not ourselves'.

I often wonder how many women of my age still think it is
purely wicked to think of themselves first.

But where the Brownies may have ignored the concept of
self-praise, we did not shy away from praising God. Oh gosh,
quite the opposite. Loving the Lord went hand in hand with
toadstool pirouetting, and my Brownie pack were smilingly
coerced just before the weekend into going to church the
following Sunday at 9 a.m. As a Bishop Goodwin Primary
School child I was well primed in God's mysterious ways, but
this was next level.

I began rising early for church and soon began confirmation
lessons so I could taste the blood of Christ at communion and
all that palaver. And why not? This Jesus, with his good deeds
and magic tricks, sounded a decent enough fella. Be nice to

everyone, he says! Sing hosannah for the king of kings! And say thank you to God who gave us his only son ... and then let him die, except not really, because Jesus was only kidding and leapt up again from the tomb, shouting, 'HALLO, FOOLED YOU ALL!' and this was all further proof of how much God loved us.

Something like that anyway.

I found these bits of church really confusing.

The very best thing about church was the coffee morning afterwards, where a small industrious troop of ladies laid out a table with slices of Madeira cake, jammy dodgers and sometimes even a Bakewell tart. This made it worth going.

Around now, despite being merely a stubby little thing with scabbed knees poking out of a sixth-hand Brownie tunic, I was experiencing a subtle awakening on class.

On every third Sunday of the month, the most shining glory was awarded to one of us: the chance to carry our bright-yellow flag up the aisle at church, during 'parade'.

Here, as one of the stars of the show, you would parade side by side with key members of the Boys' Brigade and Currock Girl Guides. The Guides were so impossibly chic I trembled in their presence. They wore neat navy shirts with a pencil skirt, navy-blue bonnet hats and forty-denier tights. Through the congregation, made up largely of sour-faced OAPs, local businessowners and people nudged towards God by their Alcoholics Anonymous meeting, you'd walk up the aisle hoisting your flag. Then, to a tuneless rendition of 'To Be a Pilgrim', it was placed behind the altar by the vicar, who asked God to bless our pack for another month.

Flag-carrying was a role I was never, ever given.

We were all normal, everyday sort of people where I came from. We were all more or less the same. Except I was starting to suspect that maybe sometimes we weren't. There were tiny, subtle differences. Some of us were better, a bit fancier, and I had my suspicions that, in the eyes of Brown Owl at least, I was a bit common. Brown Owl, in real life, was a woman called Joyce who lived in a detached house, drove a Ford Cortina with a National Trust sticker and was once spotted by my mother in our newsagent's buying the *Telegraph*. She had her card marked as 'up herself'.

Brown Owl was not supposed to have favourites, but I knew I did not make her eyes light up like, say, Darlene Phillips. Lovely Darlene, with her long legs, blonde bob and nose smattered with freckles – evidence of her family's two-week Canvas camping holiday in France. 'Camping? *Pghghg*, lying in a bloody tent being feasted on by bugs,' my mam tutted when I asked if we could go to Brittany instead of Pontins, Weston-super-Mare.

Darlene's life was much fancier than mine. Her dad was a builder, and by this I mean an actual builder, not just someone with a spirit level conning the dole. Her dad built them a breakfast bar – with tall barstools to sit at – and he designed and hammered up a lean-to on the back for their washing machine, which Darlene loftily called 'the utility room'. And she had her own SodaStream at home.

An actual SodaStream.

She sat at her breakfast bar drinking SodaStream Dandelion & Burdock in tall glasses with a scoop of vanilla ice cream. When we did our Cookery badge she brought all her ingredients in Tupperware and carried it to the hall in a wicker basket. I brought mine in a crumpled Lennards carrier bag full of old ice-cream cartons. What dismayed me most of all was that Darlene was a natural type of pretty; whereas by the age of nine I was already wondering how I might improve. Just a dab of my mother's blusher on my cheek gave a defined cheekbone, I found. A touch of pale-blue shadow on my lids made my eyes bluer. Darlene's mother, a gossipy type who came to church each week, once took Brown Owl to the side and tipped her off about my tinted lip-gloss. It's not right, she said, that a girl that age should look so much like a little tart.

'How can you decorate your Christingle orange with sweets when you've *eaten* all your sweets, Grace Dent?' asks Brown Owl as I sit beside an empty Revels packet with my cheeks distended like a pre-autumn hamster.

We are making Christingle oranges. I am trying extremely hard to symbolise God's fruits on earth by attaching a packet of Revels to an orange with cocktail sticks, but it's a shambles. This is the wrong sweet for the job.

The whole point of Revels is that they are a random assort-ment: the Malteser one, the coconut one, the orange cream and the coffee one that has to be a joke as it tastes of armpits.

Revels are a surprise each time. Christingle is a task that needs definites. I haven't thought this through.

At least I've got my ribbon wrapped around the orange, representing Christ's blood, which he shed to save us.

Darlene Phillips's Christingle orange is perfect.

It has a perfect red ribbon around the centre. It is festooned with midget gems on cocktail sticks, representing Mother Nature's abundance. She has scooped a hole out of the top and pushed in a candle to symbolise Jesus, 'who is the light of the world'.

'Darlene really is so good with arts and crafts,' says Brown Owl proudly. 'She should take *her* orange up to the Reverend Kevin at the Christingle Ceremony.'

I push the last of the Revels into my gob and seethe. Darlene is always up at that flipping altar with the flag and her mother cheering her on. The Son, the Father and the Holy Ghost must be sick of the bloody sight of her.

1980

'Worrya doin', precious?' my dad says, looking over his *Evening News* as I clamber up the back of the sofa, attempting to fish an object off the top of the dresser in our living room. I've been told off for this at least sixty times and warned it'll topple over and kill me. It went in one ear, out the other.

'I'm just gerrinthisbutton off the dresser,' I tell Dad, mirroring his scouse lilt.

'Whah button?' he says.

'The one that fell off me school blouse,' I say. 'Mam purrit up here to keep it safe.'

'Mam'll go wild about you climbin' on that settee in yer shoes,' he tells me.

Dad is not quite telling me off; he is merely pointing out the inevitability of my mother's ire. It is a technique he uses throughout my life.

'Oh yeah,' I say, remembering that I am wearing my Polyveldts; a pair of chunky treated-leather monstrosities that Mam has bought me and David. She cannot afford to keep up with our rate of destroying shoes. Polyveldts – a hybrid of moccasins and trainers – will survive the rough and tumble of Bishop Goodwin life. We hate them but have agreed to wear them 'until they wear out'. This was sheer folly on our part, as Polyveldts do not ever wear out. They are unkillable.

I sit down on the couch and take a small empty Lion matchbox from my grey school cardigan pocket. I open it and pop the button inside.

'Worrayou up to?' he says.

I sigh in a defeated manner.

Last week's take-home task at Brownies was to find an empty matchbox – a small one like any of us would have around the house – and see how many little tiny items we could cram inside. And the winner would get a prize!

'How about', Brown Owl hinted, 'if you took a grain of pudding rice? Or a tiny dried pea? Or you folded down the wrapper off an Opal Fruit?'

We stared at her in wonder.

'So next week's winner will get these,' she said, producing a small box of Terry's Harlequin.

'Wow,' we all gasped, ignoring the fact that these chocolates had clearly been hanging around her house a bit, as the corner of the box had been gnawed by her golden retriever, Clement.

Dad has put down his *Evening News & Star* and is stood up, peering into one of the drawers on the dresser.

'There's a tiny nut and bolt in here I saved off your roller skate,' he says.

He retrieves it and then unscrews the small, delicate fastener from the tiny bolt. He plops them both inside the matchbox.

'Two things!' I say.

'Yeah, two things. The nut and the bolt count as two. Don't be tellin' Brown Owl that nut was ever attached to that bolt or she might count it as just one.'

Dad's ethos in life was always that rules were for bending. And that you can get away with anything if no one finds out.

We add three more things to the matchbox:

The corner of a 67 bus ticket from Five Road Ends,
    Currock, to the Town Hall.
A piece of thread off the hem of my dad's work sock.
An apple pip we find on the floor, both rolling our eyes in
    agreement that my mam's hoovering skills can't be up to
    much. We'll mention her slackness to her when she
    returns from driving Grandad to dominos at the Working
    Men's Club and has got all our teas on.

'OK, let's see what we can find in the kitchen,' he says.

(It's funny how those magical moments that parents strive to create for their children very often make no impact at all. Daytrips to theme parks, Christmas pantomime afternoons, trips to the zoo; they can pass without much joy. But I remember vividly standing on a chair, shoulder to shoulder with my father, rooting through the kitchen cupboard in joint determination to win the matchbox game.)

We add to my tiny haul:

A tiny dehydrated pea from a Bachelors Barbecue Bacon & Tomato Cup-a-Soup.

A tiny piece of dehydrated carrot.

A grain of long-grain rice.

A grain of tapioca pudding rice.

A Whiskas duck and liver cat biscuit.

A red lentil my mam put in pressure cookers of Scotch broth.

A corner of foil from an Oxo cube.

A corner of a Smith's Salt 'n' Shake salt packet.

A hundred and thousand from a Birds Trifle.

The toe of a Pickled Onion Monster Munch.

Eventually, after some rooting around down the back of the sofa and in the lean-to at the back of the house, we have pushed twenty-eight items into the matchbox, cramming them in until the tray can barely slide into its white Lion outer cover.

''Ere, don't be opening it again before you do the big count,' Dad says, 'cos we might not gerrit shut.'

'I won't,' I say.

'And don't you be letting that Brown Owl make you feel daft,' he says. 'Does she know that you're top of the class in your reading and your writing? You wanna tell her that.'

I'm not sure how I'm going to drop that into conversation, but I like that he is clearly proud.

My dad helped teach me to read at the age of four with flash-cards made from the back of cereal packets.

Cake.

Bake.

This.

That.

Tree.

It took me at least another two decades to work out how poor he was at reading and writing himself.

It took me years to realise how much he had shaped who I am. Dad taught me never to say no to paid work, even if you're snowed under, because work dries up. Dad taught me that keeping money rolling in – no matter what – and relying on no one is the most upstanding thing a person can do. Dad taught me that no one is indispensable; never think you are above being replaced – perfect advice, though it wasn't his intention, for a career in media. The story he used to demon-strate this, which he told me often, involved one of his friends when he was a young man in the REME, who accidentally shot himself through the head one weekend in the barracks. The following Monday morning everyone was very sad, until about lunchtime when all the man's tasks were redistributed and no one mentioned him again. It took me at least three decades to work out that his friend had not accidentally killed himself. Dad also taught me that work is a fantastic place to hide. Head down, chop-chop, keep busy, keep working: you can keep on running from yourself.

I have been finding tiny items to stuff in the matchbox for days. Rooting in drawers, opening folders, putting my face in places I really shouldn't. I have been looking at two photos I have found stored in an envelope and reading letters that are not for my eyes. Some things I have seen are very confusing. I have found a black-and-white photo of two little girls in my father's bedside drawer. Two happy little girls. Smiling and waving. I do not know who they are. I will not mention them to anyone for many years. My dad taught me that everyone has secrets. He taught me that no one is ever truly knowable. Dad taught me that everybody – and I mean everybody – fibs.

I skip to Brownies the following evening, quietly confident that I am in with a chance of winning, because me and my dad have properly put the graft in over this.

As all the little Brownies gather round the trestle table in the Methodist Hall clutching their Lion matchboxes, a whisper begins to grow throughout the pack that Darlene has forty-five items inside hers.

'Forty-five?' I say.

'But her matchbox is different,' says Tracy Fitzackerly.

'*How* is it different?' I say.

'Her matchbox is sort of longer,' Tracy says, not seeming overly fussed as she's only stuffed ten items in hers anyway.

I walk down the table to find Darlene Phillips holding a neatly packed-to-the-brim yellow Swan Vestas matchbox.

Some girls are muttering that this doesn't seem fair. The Swan Vestas box is much larger than a normal box. We all had to have the same size box. Brown Owl, who looks ruffled at first, is now saying she did not specify which type of matchbox we could use. Also, if you think about it, Darlene's box is not as deep, so that makes everything fair. People seem to bend the rules for girls like Darlene. It's like anything is possible.

'I don't think this is fair,' mutters Tracey Fitzackerly.

'Oh Darlene, that is very clever,' says Brown Owl. 'Jesus is in there too!'

Brown Owl is thrilled that as Darlene opens the box, a tiny gold crucifix is inside among the other items. A tiny Jesus on the cross, borrowed from Darlene's mum's necklace.

'Isn't that marvellous,' says Brown Owl.

'It's a bigger box,' I say audibly.

'No, it isn't, Grace,' says Brown Owl. 'They're the same size.'

Somehow I manage *not* to say some of the best swearwords in my nine-year-old cursing artillery. I do not say 'piss' or 'arse' or the bizarrely effective showstopper 'twat'.

I do not say any of that.

I don't say anything.

I stand quietly, inwardly bubbling, as Darlene Phillips is given the box of Terry's Harlequin.

And then, in the final minutes of the meeting, Darlene is made Sixer of the Pixies and is given her silver lapel badge.

I find my BHS ski jacket under the pile of other coats, pull it on over my Brownie uniform and skulk home alone.

As I reach the Five Road Ends I see my dad in Donny's chip shop, fetching everyone's tea. I tell him what went on. He hugs me into the armpit of his work jersey. It smells of sweat and WD-40.

'Oh, presh,' he says. 'Bugger thalorro'them.'

And then he buys me a pickled egg.

Life, I was starting to see, was really not fair and some people simply had a much smoother ride than others.

That said, seven years later, when Darlene Phillips had a surprise baby in their utility room, then wrapped it in a towel and handed it to her mother after she kicked the door down, everyone at church was completely scandalised.

Except for me.

I thought it was really, really funny.

My mother is pushing a small rickety shopping trolley with a wobbly back wheel down a narrow aisle at Presto supermarket on Botchergate, Carlisle. She's trying to do the big Friday shop between five o'clock and half past six, leaving enough time to drive across the city, drop off odds and ends to my gran, spin back, unload our car, then make everyone's teas before my dad gets narky.

'He won't think to make his own,' she says.

Being a mam never looks like very much fun. I am starting to have notions that I do not want babies of my own.

Even as a toddler, on being handed a Tiny Tears doll I was slightly flummoxed as to the point of it all.

'Look, she cries,' my mam said, 'so you pick her up to cuddle her. And she wees herself so you can change her nappy!'

It was fun for half an hour.

Grocery shopping, however, felt more like a fun game. By modern standards, Presto was little more than a mini-mart – as big as a couple of tennis courts – but in 1980 it was one of the largest places in Cumbria to buy groceries. It even had a multi-storey car park with exciting concrete ramps. My mother never seemed more like a warrior than when she was jamming the accelerator on her Austin Princess and speeding up the steep entry ramp, yelling, 'Weeeeeeeeee!'

There were very few men in the supermarket.

Women in cream tabards ran the tills, stacked the shelves and cut and weighed out slices of that spooky pork luncheon tongue slab with the boiled egg lurking inside. Women roamed the aisles, peering at shopping lists, trying to make house-keeping stretch a full seven days, pleading for their kids' patience but inevitably losing them in the aisles. Leaving your kids at home alone became very much 'not the done thing' in the 1980s. A cacophony of ghoulish public-safety ads played on Border TV during all daytime ad breaks, warning mothers that slipping out to the shops was hazardous. Within moments of popping out to get bread we would drink bleach, drown in slurry or climb electricity pylons. Presto's tannoy system rang incessantly with news of missing or found kids. Being one of the found kids, I learned quickly, was actually rather exciting. You sometimes even got a biscuit. Sometimes I'd lose myself purposefully, taking right turns and wrong turns along the aisles, merely for the thrill of sitting in the petty cash office in Lennards hearing my name being read out.

'We have a little girl here who is lost called Grace. She is three years old.'

This was my first taste of fame and I loved it.

My mother found it less jolly. Once, in Woolworths, after being reunited with me by the Pick 'n' Mix, she grabbed me, turned me round and smacked my arse as passers-by begged for clemency. This story, which is now part of Dent folklore, is always told humorously, but I can't help but think that it was not remotely funny at the time, when Mam was struggling with two kids under three.

My little brother had arrived very quickly after me. Me in October 1973, him in May 1975.

'I still have no bloody idea where he came from,' my mother has often remarked. 'I could hardly stand your dad for most of 1974.'

But I have a pretty good idea. My father was swarthily handsome. He was witty and devil-may-careish in a world of dour-faced, rule-abiding Cumbrians.

He was Lee Hazlewood to her Nancy Sinatra.

They fought like hell, due to his moods and her big plans, but never fell out for that long.

By the age of nine I was at least useful on the big Friday shop.

'Box of Daz,' she'd say, and off I'd run to the washing-powder aisle.

'Two tins of peach slices,' she'd say. 'And a tin of Tip Top.'

Back I came, with an extra Heinz Treacle Sponge Pudding under my arm. The one you pierced with a tin opener, then steamed in a pan of boiling water. Sticky, satisfying, delicious.

'Yeah, shove it in,' she'd nod.

That nod was the best thing ever.

Supermarkets made me happy.

I liked the methodology of filling the trolley, trying not to squash the bread or bruise the fruit. I liked the set-in-stone way that supermarkets always seemed to be laid out: fresh fruit and veg aisles giving way to tinned fruits and dried packets, then shampoos, then toilet paper, then wonderful-smelling washing detergents and then finally booze and tins of cat meat.

The Heinz steamed pudding, I knew by the age of nine, would come in handy for a quick after-tea pudding. Each grocery we bought at this stage had a roughly assigned purpose. We didn't buy willy-nilly. The small tin of Heinz Vegetable Salad was to go with the curly lettuce and the tin of red salmon for the 4 p.m. high tea when Gran came over on a Sunday. The tin of Smedley's Marrowfat Peas was for fishfingers and mashed potatoes on a Tuesday night. I still adore fat, squashy, slightly bland tinned Marrowfat peas, even if nowadays they've been eclipsed in the public's heart by trendy takes on mushy peas. I learned a deep respect for things out of tins early on; tinned macaroni cheese on white toast with ketchup will always cheer me up. Eating cold beans with a spoon from the tin will forever be one of my least attractive habits.

Choice, when shopping in the early Eighties, was limited. If you wanted tinned spaghetti, orange squash or raspberry jam, there were often only two sorts: supermarket brand or the posh one you'd seen on telly that your mam wouldn't let you buy.

'Shut up, it's all out of the same factory,' my mother would yell, as me and Dave begged for Robinsons Lemon Barley Water like Björn Borg drank at Wimbledon. ''Ere, this one is nice,' she'd add, loading in the Presto Mixed Fruit Squash.

The Dents' trolley contained virtually no spice, heat or evidence at all that Britain was part of the global commonwealth. Or that we even had much to do with Europe. We fried in White Cap lard. We ate Presto medium-sliced, slightly plasticky white bread. Our cheese was orange, almost always Cheddar, and we were still cagey about the idea of melting it. Rice was always white and it was used almost exclusively for puddings, which my mother would make in the oven in a glass dish. But, despite these narrow horizons, watching *Ivor the Engine* at 5.50 p.m. on a cold autumn night with a bowl of Mam's rice pudding on my knee is one of my happiest memories of all.

The lack of choice back then only made the sparkly, frivolous things off the telly that we were allowed all the more magical in my mind. The box of Nesquik Banana Milkshake powder we were allowed to mark the start of the summer holidays. The occasional box of Cadbury's chocolate zoo animals sneaked into the trolley but given the 'OK' nod. The tension along Harold Street as we waited for one of our mothers to cave in and buy Birds Eye Supermousse: sweet strawberry-and-vanilla-flavoured goo, in a small pot, with a brightly coloured cardboard lid. Those adverts played from 4 p.m. every evening and every fifteen minutes on Saturday mornings. Our small, determined hearts and minds were hostages to Kellogg's, Rowntree's, Smith's Crisps and Wall's. If you could sweet-talk a Sara Lee gateau or a bottle of Bird's Ice Magic onto that conveyer belt on a Friday, you were one of life's winners. Although more likely was that your mam would discover all those items you'd sneaked into the trolley when she got to the tills and hit the roof. Cue: more screaming, more smacked arses.

Primary school started so well for me. As one of the top kids in our class, I learned my times tables by heart and was doing joined-up writing when the others were still peering at vowels. I galloped through the Griffin Pirate series, in which the Red Pirate faffs pointlessly around the Black Cliffs for sixteen arduous volumes. Outside of 'the three Rs' of reading, writing and arithmetic, I took a keen interest in the small array of completely useless topics a Seventies working-class kid was taught: fictitious hokum about the life of Robin Hood, the feeding habits of a brontosaurus (which may or may not have existed), Viking longship building and, at my school, New Testament parables – water to wine, the feeding of the five thousand, the good Samaritan and so on.

'Grace is a bright spark,' it said on my school report each term, but without any further nod to where this could lead.

It is hard, perhaps, for some younger people nowadays to understand a world where no one mentioned further education to the lower classes, ever. Not once. Not even in passing. Perhaps it feels unfeasible that this vacuum of ambition or aspiration could possibly exist. But it did. The only thing I wanted to be when I grew up was glamorous. This was within my power. I wanted to be really, really glamorous. Like Margi Clarke in *Letter to Brezhnev*. Or Joanne from The Human League in the 'Don't You Want Me' video in an ankle-length mink coat. Or Alexis Colby in *Dynasty* striding from a helicopter to push Blake's annoying second wife Krystal into the koi carp pond, again. Glamorous was something I could get my teeth into. It was there on the telly on *Coronation Street* or the Miss World competition.

Still, despite doing well in school, by the age of eleven I'd seen almost none of the classic children's books that make those broadsheet '100 Best ...' lists each year: A.A. Milne, C.S. Lewis, E. Nesbit. Those tomes that apparently enrich the soul. I'd never heard of Dickens, Shakespeare or Tolkien. I knew nothing of Greek mythology or been tipped off that Latin was even a thing. The stuff you need a smattering of if you want to pass as posh.

Like most kids of my ilk, as a small child I was exposed to no foreign languages at all. And while I knew basic spelling, I was taught next to no grammar. I still feel these gaps constantly, despite incessantly trying to improve and catch up during my twenties and thirties. The difference between 'fewer' and 'less', for example, is something I only discovered in my late thirties when people sneered, 'Surely, you mean FEWER restaurants have opened, not LESS?' But that's generally always the lower middle classes, for whom pedantry is their affliction; an inability to stop pointing out minor errors in people with less bright starts, before basking for the rest of the chat in a dank pool of bad feeling. Speaking perfect grammatical English, for people with my childhood, will always be like speaking a second language near fluently. We're very impressive – and such a breath of fresh air to have around – but of course we make minor errors. That said, my primary-school days had their uses – if you want help nurturing frogspawn into tadpoles and releasing them in a patch of marshland around the back of Allied Carpets, look no further. It's a shame that even this relatively bright start soon fizzled out.

I arrived at Caldew Secondary, a state comprehensive, in 1983, at the tail end of corporal punishment, just as the teachers had been requested to stop beating the pupils with belts, canes or shoes. It was a disappointment for them, as they clearly missed it. Now, in this moribund centre of non-excellence six miles outside of Carlisle, the powers of this old guard of angry male tutors were sorely reduced. Shouting was their only option. The corridors rocked with their stale-breathed impotent threats. Hurling kids out of class, out of sight, out of mind was a chief tactic to deal with the troublesome. While a small sixth form catered for the more promising handful after the age of sixteen, until then you were part of a one-thousand-strong mob. There had been no grammar-school option to spirit me away to more promising climes – not that the eleven-plus exam had done my family any favours. Both my parents had failed it. My mother – bright as a button – went to a secondary modern and by fourteen was working in a local hat shop. Now a similar fate awaited me and my little brother. My big brother Bob had left school at fifteen and, after a few futile Youth Training Schemes, had packed a bag and left for London with friends. He told us in a letter he was working washing dishes.

I missed Bob a lot. His dad was my mam's first husband, she explained delicately when I was about seven. This made no odds to me: he was my brother and that was that. After he left, the house was much more boring. I missed the sound of David Bowie coming from under his rude remarks about Margaret Thatcher – Bob wasn't a fan like Mam was. I loved him bringing home videos for me to puzzle over, like *Monty Python and the Holy Grail*. Bob was funny and brave; he dyed his hair wild colours, rode a Vespa scooter and would travel to other towns to go to nightclubs with his friends. Mam and my dad were always furious at him for not 'sticking in' at his latest job creation scheme at a carpet warehouse or a gent's barber. The fights about his hair, his nocturnal hours and 'Maggie' were loud and endless. Then one weekend Bob left. He gave me a turntable and a copy of *Parallel Lines* by Blondie. He moved to Kilburn and then to a squat in Manor House. No one could tell him what to do anymore. One day, I will run away too, I thought.

The 1980s British comp-school education was a rudimentary affair. I learned French language for five years from a woman with a broad Carlisle accent who I am now unsure ever set foot in France. '*Uhhhhn sandweeeech, seel voooz play,*' we'd all repeat, sharing Tricolore text books full of scenes of everyday life in La Rochelle. The French were weird; they couldn't even buy a lump of cheese without a three-hour round trip on a *bicyclette* to a specialist *fromagerie*. The French made a right fuss of food. It seemed bizarre to me. They spent three hours having dinner, as they wanted to chat to each other and enjoy their food. Absolute madness, I thought.

By the age of thirteen, I was already predicted to leave school without a maths GCSE. No teachers made any attempt to explain that a university application form in the 1980s needed a maths GCSE as an absolute minimum requirement, plus at least one GCSE in a science like chemistry, biology or physics. Instead, to worsen matters, I was chivvied towards a qualification called modular science: a sort of holding pen for children too frightening to be allowed near Bunsen burners.

In modular science our teachers attempted to explain difficult concepts like rainbows, before inevitably pinching the soft skin between their eyes and letting us draw a rainbow instead. In absolute fairness to the science department, I can't blame them for giving up on us. I'd been brought up loving the Lord, who created all things heaven and earth in six days and spent the seventh watching *Bullseye* and drinking Kia-Ora. I had no interest in anything as unfeasible as physics. When Heston Blumenthal shows up making a risotto with a Dyson Airblade and a conical flask of formaldehyde, I still think: Use a pan, mate. Stop dicking about.

Lessons began to leave me behind. I loved swinging on my chair at the back, surrounded by a mob dissecting last night's *Top of the Pops*. I loved doing impressions of popstars or making up song lyrics. Words were my one strength: daft poems, song words, nicknames. Finding joy in the mundane. In fact, the very same things that pay my mortgage now. But then, as a difficult pupil – gobby, booby, easily distracted by anything in Insignia body spray – I made a natural ally for the kids in King Kurt T-shirts who liked setting fire to stuff and locking staff in cupboards. To our credit, we always let them out in the end.

So, by fourteen, despite being a shining star at infant school, I was quite patently out of the running for Oxford or Cambridge. Or Durham, Manchester, Cardiff, Leeds or, for that matter, any of the tried-and-tested routes to where actual power lay in the 1980s. This story is not remotely unusual. It is absolutely bog-standard, Grade-A humdrum. Being bright but working class in Eighties Britain was a huge game of snakes and ladders. You could ascend for a while, but a few bad choices here and there and down you'd go again. Thankfully, in that era, Carlisle still had industry. Pupils who left school at sixteen could pack mint Viscounts at Carr's biscuit factory or count pies off the conveyer belt at Cavaghan & Gray, and there was always a job at the Southwaite service station on the M6 clearing tables. The good thing about these jobs was the ten-till-three shift option, which you could fit around picking up kids, and then grandkids, from the school gate.

My one joy at school was home economics, where I mastered toad in the hole and the incredibly chic party canapé stuffed boiled eggs (the innards mixed with salad cream and Cheddar). At Christmas I perfected yule log by smearing a Co-op chocolate Swiss roll with a rudimentary 'ganache' made of Stork SB and hot-chocolate powder. Home economics was the only lesson where my teacher's eyes actually lit up at my 'panache'. I had panache. My chicken and tinned pineapple skewer was praised hugely both for presentation and seasoning – even if Dad did look a bit green around the gills on the twelfth occasion he got it for tea afterwards. At least here was a class where I could shine.

But when I think about secondary school now, I never think of learning at all. I think of crowded corridors, the arch cruelty of kids and, from just before noon every lunchtime, the uplifting aroma of gravy.

* * *

'What's that up your sleeve, sonny Jim?' screamed Haggis, the school dinner lady.

The small boy shuddered in fear.

'Is that an iced bun? Gimme that bun. Gimme it!'

Caldew's head dinner supervisor was a terrifying lady from Scotland who we called – with great ingenuity – Haggis Basher.

She was six foot two, broad-chested like a sergeant major, with a curly mop of black hair and a voice like an angry velociraptor. If Roald Dahl had created Haggis for one of his books, he would have probably edited her out of the final draft as a touch unbelievable. Her greatest obsession was the school rule 'No food items are to be consumed outside the hall'. Haggis, who had at least six sets of eyes, some definitely on her back, adhered to this rule with great tenacity.

'You can get this bun back tomorrow!' she shouted, snatching the boy's sticky baked treat (which he'd hoped to enjoy on the playing field) and plopping it into her tabard pocket. As good as her word, Haggis would give him that bun back the next day at noon – squashed and with washing-machine lint tangled in the icing.

Haggis ran the hall like a military manoeuvre because – I see now only with hindsight – hurtling one thousand children, in three sittings, through a dining hall in seventy minutes is no small task.

Every day she delivered nothing short of a gastronomical miracle.

Three sittings, three hundred kids at a time, fed by a squadron of fierce women in duck-egg-blue tabards flinging beige, battered and breadcrumbed items out of a hatch in the wall. Dinner consisted of three stainless-steel terrines of mushy, lukewarm, delicious chips sat close to warm jugs of lumpy, powder-based gravy. There were fearsome fist-sized breadcrumbed balls of mashed potato and diced ham known as 'rissoles' and square slices of 'vegetable pizza' – spongey white bread strewn with diced carrots, runner beans and melted cut-price Cheddar. Those Turkey Twizzlers that upset Jamie Oliver so greatly were yet to be invented, but instead we had ominous burgers and cheap hot-dog sausages, which were 20 per cent salt water, 80 per cent pig's lips and bumholes. Prices for all these things were rock bottom: for sixty pence a day you could eat like a king. Albeit a king who might have died quite young from scurvy.

To be fair, health and wellness were not ignored completely. There were jacket potatoes – never with fancy fillings, mind; just the potato. The true sophisticate ate theirs smeared with sachets of ketchup. And for the very stiff-nerved fitness freak, there was salad. Well, to be exact, three salads – that's three pre-made salads to cater for one thousand pupils. They were plated up, cling-filmed over and placed by the chips. But, by Christ, it would be a raffish, vagabond child who'd touch one of these la-dee-dah fucking school-swot salad plates of chopped iceberg, grated carrot, boiled egg and a few dessert-spoons of canned sweetcorn. Salad was one of those things a posh person like Penny from *Just Good Friends* might eat. And as kids, the majority of us were desperate to never, ever stand out. Standing out was suicidal.

Haggis needed to keep us all eating inside the hall because no sane person wanted to linger there: it was a hotspot for bullying. If we'd had our way, most of us would have bought food and fled, scattering crumbs and ketchup through the yard. This was the era of proper old-fashioned Eighties face-to-face school bullying. The more headbanger kids at our school took a pride in their daily visitations. The school pond was full of dumped satchels, the toilets were perpetually blocked with coats and matron's office perpetually full of sick children who were actually hiding. Secondary school affected how millions of British children felt about other human beings forever. Home-schooled children are a liability in the workplace and in social groups; they are naive, malleable and overly trusting, because they didn't ever learn at school how awful people can be.

I got off semi-lightly, in as much as I was called a slag or an ugly cow by older girls at least every other day. This was just normal and, if anything, I was being provocative. My half-decent posture was definite evidence of supposing I was 'it'. Reckoning you were 'it' in Eighties working-class Britain was a grave crime. It required almost no evidence to prosecute; a confident manner, a new ski jacket, some shoes with a fancy toe cap all constituted putting your head above the parapet in some way.

And in the lunch hall, all our differences were laid bare.

I say differences with a caveat: we were one thousand Caucasian children raised in the Church of England faith. Our backgrounds were as uniformly beige as our lunch plates.

None of us had the sheer brass neck to be openly gay, bi, queer or trans. A 'tranny' was something your Uncle Brian might borrow to do a twenty-four-hour booze-buying trip to Calais. None of our parents were especially rich, poor, smothering, feral or absent. Our uniformity only made the bullying more innovative. By my second year at 'big school', I had learned – rather depressingly – that when Joanne from the year above sent a message wanting a fight, the pragmatic option was to walk directly over to Joanne by the chips, grab her by the demi-wave and drag her backwards past the millionaire's shortbread with her skirt riding up so everyone could see her pants. Clever retorts did not work with these people. It is no accident that so few of the working classes go on to choose a life on the debating circuit and choose hobbies like cage fighting instead.

With all this in mind, perhaps it's unsurprising how the working classes have such a soft spot for that type of school-dinner pudding that they remember making their day feel slightly better – like sweet, cheaply made apple crumble with custard or honking square lumps of chocolate sponge smothered in some sort of pink creamy sauce. I'd dispatch a sainthood to whichever culinary genius invented Australian Crunch, crushed cornflakes, desiccated coconut, cheap margarine, sugar and cocoa-flavoured powder churned into a traybake and topped with thick melted cooking chocolate.

School dinners were where an entire generation of working-class kids learned that beige food is a blanket of happiness to snuggle around you on an otherwise shitty school day. This stays with many of us for life. After a woeful day dealing with dickheads at work, very few people experience a guttural yearning for a bowl of mixed leaves with oil-free dressing.

No.

Give me a chip butty covered in vinegar and so much salt I can feel my heart valves clogging. Give me pizza so inauthentic that it would make a Neapolitan weep. Give me food that helps in the short term but in the long term reduces my lifespan.

When Jamie Oliver finally went to war on school dinners and what mothers fed their kids back in 2005, I couldn't help thinking: God love him, his heart's in the right place, but he has no idea what he is taking on. These mothers were my age group, they'd lived my life. Oliver was on a hiding to nothing, telling them a plate of broccoli was a lunch option for their little Lee-Reuben. Even when he managed to ban the Twizzlers, some mams came to the school and pushed emergency Happy Meals through the school fence. It looked shocking, I know, but I understood. They just wanted their kids to be fed and happy.

By the age of fourteen, a division was growing between me and my father.

He could not protect me from Caldew or possibly understand how it felt for me growing up.

He left the heavy lifting of all my hormonal teenage stroppiness to my mother. And as I grew curvier, bolshier, more belligerent and less likely to show my face at school five days in a row, my father hid away from our arguments. I turned my mother's hair silver with anger. I told every lie I could dream up to stay at home and read Jackie Collins novels in bed. Sore throats, bad heads, heavy periods, imaginary teacher training days. Sometimes just plain old-fashioned screaming 'I'm not bloody going!'

All this was nobody else's fault but my own.

Fourteen-year-old girls in the 1980s were a law unto themselves. We did not consider ourselves to be children.

We read *Cosmopolitan* magazine cover to cover and loved the articles on stronger, harder orgasms. We pooled our pocket money and bought Thunderbird or Merrydown cider or Kestrel lager to drink in the bogs at school discos. We stole Cinzano Bianco from our mothers' drinks' cabinets and knocked it back neat with a Feminax period pain pill to get us more dizzily drunk. We danced to 'Rebel Yell' by Billy Idol or 'Blue Monday' by New Order or 'Male Stripper' by Man 2 Man and we had sex in our grandparents' seaside static caravans or standing up in bus shelters and it was all bloody brilliant. The pubs served us vodka and lime without question and we went to nightclubs without even needing fake ID, just with false birthdays and star signs memorised. We drank snakebite and black or shots of Dubonnet and pints of Caffrey's and long vodkas made with Rose's Lime Juice Cordial and Angostura bitters. We doused ourselves in Anaïs Anaïs by Cacherel and had older boyfriends with Sun-In-streaked mullets who drove Ford Fiesta XR2s and Escort Mk 3s, who would get banged up in young offenders' institutes for low-level soccer hooliganism. We had boyfriends who smoked bongs and listened to AC/DC who were scaffolders and picked us up from school in their Ford Capri to drive us home.

The word grooming was just something posh girls did with their ponies.

We smoked Regal King Size, which we stole from our nans. We wore our school skirts rolled over at the waistline with Pineapple boxer boots and neon fishnet tights and Rimmel Heather Shimmer lipstick and we tried to hide the lovebites on our necks with Constance Carroll concealer stick, although we were secretly proud of them, especially the ones on our boobs. We put ourselves on the pill at the local family planning clinic (carting along random willing teenage boys to play the parts of steady, responsible boyfriends), which the nurses dished out with grateful abandon, because they knew the alternative was that many would fake consent forms to book abortions, which in a time before computerised records was as easy as pie.

And we did all this without many tears.

It didn't occur to us that we were victims.

We were Generation X, raised without playdates, allergies, safe spaces and CRB checks, when getting your tits felt up – not entirely consensually – at the back of the Manchester Free Trade Hall was, we reckoned, the best part of going to see Spacemen 3. It was a world before TikTok, before cameras in every pocket, before it felt imperative to capture, log and broadcast every experience in order to harvest attention.

Teenagers in the Eighties knew the value of discretion.

Of sworn-to-the-heart secrecy.

Of sneaking about.

And we generally got away with it. And now that Generation X are the parents, we pretend none of it happened at all.

My dad stayed right out of most of this. He buried himself in work and tried hard not to be there at tea time. Thatcherism was working out beautifully for some portions of society – much less so for others – but for him it brought a new way to earn money. With consumerism on the rise, he bought a white Ford Escort van and set himself up as a delivery driver. He acquired a hard-luck-story Alsatian puppy with a black ear whom he called Cilla, who sat in the front seat guarding the goods. People needed more stuff – white goods, home office supplies, even the occasional computer – and now my dad worked night and day to deliver them, never refusing a job.

Dad was happiest when he and Cilla were on the motorway driving away from the fights in our living room. Driving away from the television that never played what he wanted anymore but was now showing 'that clown' Morrissey spinning with a handful of gladioli, Michael Hutchence in bike shorts 'acting like a poof' or endless episodes of *Airwolf* while me and David gave each other dead arms.

He found family life – being the one supposedly in charge – no fun at all. My mother took up the slack.

That said, he had very limited experience of being a good example. And his sins had only just come back to haunt him.

CHAPTER 2

A Galaxy Far, Far Away

October 1988

'Can no one bloody help me with these bags?' my mother shouts, standing beside the car boot.

I'm on the sofa. I'm aged fifteen.

I'm pretty busy writing a stinging letter on Basildon Bond notepaper to Steven Wells, aka 'Swells', at the *NME* who runs the letters page. I've recently had one printed – a glowing epistle about the Pixies. Seeing my name in print has felt like a shaft of celestial light bringing joy into my moody teen world. My name. In the *NME*. I've not told anyone at home as I'm a bit embarrassed. The words – extolling the wonders of Kim Deal – feel so naked and exposing. Anyone can read them. But the exposure is also addictive. I'm writing to Swells again about Throwing Muses, hoping to chance my luck.

The letters page was often my favourite part of any magazine. I'd written continuously to 'Black Type' in *Smash Hits*, the mysterious figure who edited the readers' correspondence. His style was deeply irreverent and made an enormous mark on my sense of humour. Black Type's replies were mainly

faux-outrage and absurdity peppered with a string of nicknames for popstars that pricked their egos: Paul 'Fab Macca
Wacky Thumbs Aloft' McCartney and 'Sir Billiam of Idol'. I
imagined the office was like a huge party and that by writing
I might get invited. But that never happened, so now I was
chancing my arm with the *NME*.

Mam's voice gets angrier.

'*Uggggggh*,' I grunt, and punch David on the arm. 'It's
your turn.' He's watching *You Bet!* with Bruce Forsyth.
Neither of us are available for menial work.

David kicks me back.

'She's shouting at you too.'

We both rise and stumble out of the house in the rain over
the concrete driveway.

As a van driver my dad earned more than he ever did as
a squaddie, a stacker driver or a security guard. We were
not by any standards rich, but we were a little better off
than we were. This meant one big thing to my mam: a better
house.

The Dents had moved up in the world. OK, sort of sideways. My mam wanted more space and soon she had her eye
on an odd, cavernous, detached doer-upper going for a
bargain price close to our terrace. Our new house on
Southdale Street dated back to the seventeenth century, some
people thought. It should've probably, on reflection, been a
listed building, if anyone in Carlisle had cared about that type
of thing. But no one did, because Carlisle was swimming in
old stuff. We were knee-deep in relics and artefacts. We bull-

dozed quaint Elizabethan vennels and built Laser Quests and Yates's Wine Lodges. It was called progress.

Mam, in a similar manner, was not prepared to tiptoe around anything as creatively stifling as 'original features'. After all our belongings had been moved in – not by professional movers, just by us carrying them ourselves, looking like a mobile circus – we wondered how long it would be before the changes began.

It wasn't long. She had someone tear out supporting walls, hammer up MDF and pebble-dash the outside walls. She ordered a burgundy bathroom suite, Artex-swirled the ceilings herself and divided the walls with fake paper dado rails. She built a Venetian-inspired patio area outside for her rotary dryer and gnomes. She bought plantation fans and decorated the hallway with weeping Pierrot clown pictures and red-framed prints of elegant geishas. We were increasingly fancy.

Sadly, Mother's aim to be posh was thwarted at each turn by our next-door neighbours, who were resolutely common. Mam was uncharmed by their Shetland pony Pegasus, which grazed on dandelions in their overgrown garden. It wouldn't have any luck on our side; Mam had cemented over the garden to build a driveway. Now she could park closer to the house.

'Can you at least help me with the bloody bags before you start pushing stuff down your throats?' screams my mother.

It is the greatest moment of the week.

Mam is back with the big shop.

Me and Dave retrieve precisely one grocery item each – a box of Fairy Snow and a can of spaghetti hoops – then begin rifling through the bags and troughing down Penguins, both wearing damp towelling socks.

Bliss. Mam has been on one of her intergalactic space missions to a fantastic new galaxy. The weekend has landed.

It's difficult to explain the seismic change the new ASDA superstore had on the lives of the Dent family. Or, for that matter, on Carlisle itself. Forget Princess Diana's death or the Sex Pistols on *Today* with Bill Grundy – every Carlisle person of a certain age can remember the day they set eyes on the big new ASDA. This flash, modern, enormous superstore was built on a scrap of scrubland just off the M6, five miles from the Scottish border. In fact, the Scots even began travelling into England to shop there. They couldn't resist this 34,000-square-foot grocery nirvana.

From the moment the big ASDA came, those little supermarkets – Presto, Lennards – would only ever be second best; somewhere you picked up 'a few bits'. Life was never the same once you'd swept through big ASDA's swooshing automatic doors, breathed in wafts of freshly baked, cheese-topped tiger bloomer from the in-store bakery and experienced the magical Narnia of chiller cabinets, each one crammed with at least eight different types of fish finger, burger or frozen croquette. The prices were incredible too. Forty-eight potato waffles for ninety-nine pence! Buy one, get one free!

But big ASDA wasn't just about food. Oh no.

There was a toy department too. And you could get your dry-cleaning done and pick up your NHS prescriptions and get keys cut and sit down afterwards and have a cup of tea.

On the opening day my parents went twice. The second time, I reckon, was to check they'd not imagined it.

I mean, it was almost too good to be true. This was a place where you could pop in for a pack of pork luncheon tongue and come out with a Clairol Foot Spa and a CD of Barry Manilow live in Acapulco.

Around now, shopping took on a sense of largesse for my family. After a trip to ASDA, food was piled high from the front door onwards; mountains and mountains of stuff you didn't know you needed, such as giftboxes of Ferrero Rocher, six packs of plump, glossy, American-style double-chocolate-chip muffins, crates of Tennent's Lager and twenty-four boxes of Coca-Cola. It felt silly to just buy what you needed. Especially as every evening perishable items were sold off for practically nothing. This meant something remarkable – that every day could feel like your birthday at ASDA if you loitered by the Thomas the Tank Engine celebration cakes at closing time, waiting for the appearance of one of Cumbria's most influential figures: the woman in charge of the reduced-sticker gun. This was the lady who dotted a big yellow 'Whoops!' label on each new bargain.

'Thomas the Tank cake! Get in!' shouts my brother, rifling through the big-shop bags.

'It was meant to be three quid, but we got it for forty-four pence!' my mother says, shaking her head all over again at the magic of this brave new world.

My parents' earliest memory of eating was Second World War rationing: powdered egg, sugar shortages and pooling the street's food tokens to make a wedding sponge cake. And now here they were, in the late Eighties, blindsided by choice. My parents had experienced scarcity and experienced abundance, and the latter was much lovelier. It did start to occur to me around now, however, that maybe everything was not as rosy as it seemed. It felt to me like ASDA, and later on Morrisons, which quickly opened just down the road, made shoppers feel slightly foolish for *not* wanting twenty-four reduced-price, slightly stale bleached-flour white rolls for thirty pence. These bargains were too good to miss.

'But, Mam, we don't need rolls,' I say as I unpack the bag.

'Oh, we can freeze them,' my mam says.

But our freezer is overflowing, and the trunk one she's installed in our lean-to is full too.

No one needed this much food in their house. But as our waistbands tightened and our chins multiplied, nothing was stopping us enjoying Whoops! reduced-price boxes of doughnuts. Six delicious, plump, sugar-sprinkled doughnuts for forty-eight pence. Can you believe it? Like a lot of the working classes in the Eighties, the supermarkets had made us accustomed to jam yesterday, jam today and jam tomorrow too.

When food experts sneer about supermarkets, there is a part of me – the little girl – who always feels oddly wounded.

My loyalty still run deeps. During all those shopping trips I went on during the Eighties and Nineties with my family, ASDA was our refuge. It was a place of temporary family harmony. A happy place where we could put a pin in our urge to strangle each other. For my dad, ASDA was a night out with his family without actually having to take us anywhere. Once through the front doors, the Dents would disperse in different directions. My mother would veer off towards the homeware section to look at a new pedal bin. Me, to the clothes section where the mysterious, haute-couture designer George of ASDA peddled his latest range: shiny nylon ski-pants and pastel-coloured, cap-sleeved T-shirts. Then eventually the Dents would reconvene by the tills to pack the bags together – don't squash the bread, all the tins in one bag, go and find an empty box for the bottles of wine to stand up in. Afterwards, we'd ride home together eating warm reduced-price sausage rolls with a boot full of bags and clinking bottles. We'd listen to my mother's Engelbert Humperdinck cassette, singing 'Lonely Is a Man Without Love' together with great gusto.

We were, despite our faults – and I love to remember this now – a happy family. We weren't perfect, but we had a laugh.

''Ere, I got a bottle of Bulgarian Merlot! It's 14 per cent,' my dad says when we get home, admiring his booze haul.

To my dad, strong wine means classy wine.

'We had that last time,' Mam sighs. 'It's like paint-stripper.'

'It was one pound fifty-two for two litres,' he says, unscrewing the cap.

'I'll have some, Dad,' I say, chancing my arm.

I was keen to learn about wine for when I ran away to London to become the new Paula Yates or a celebrated *NME* writer. I would definitely be drinking wine when I began hanging around London in the star-studded Groucho Club with Sigue Sigue Sputnik and Janet Street-Porter. I'd read about this type of thing in Piers 'Friend of the Stars' Morgan's 'Bizarre' column in the *Sun*.

'You can have a little drop,' he winks.

Until the late Eighties, the Dents did not buy wine. In fact, we'd hoot with glee at a lady on the telly called Jilly Goolden who would slosh it around her gob and claim she could taste babbling brooks and enchanted elderberries.

But now here we were, developing our own cosmopolitan palate. I could sneak tastes of Italian Lambrusco or Black Tower Liebfraumilch. I drank a peach-flavoured vodka called Taboo and developed a liking for Malibu coconut rum, which was *exactly* like the stuff they drank in the Caribbean, the advert said.

'She can't drink wine, George,' my mother says. 'She's fifteen.'

'A drop won't do her any harm. She's like me, she is,' says Dad. 'She's got a sophisticated palate.'

Christmas Eve, 1988

My dad is shelling Brussels sprouts. He's putting a cross at the bottom of each green cruciferous bullet with his secret good, sharp vegetable knife. It's his knife. Not mine and David's knife. We shouldn't use it. After this task he will hide it again in a kitchen drawer under a pile of old kitchen-appliance instruction booklets. As my brother and I grow older, larger, more invasive of his space, my ex-army father often treats us like pain-in-the-arse young squaddies with whom he's being forced to share barracks. He has his special knife. He has his chair. He lives in a state of constant ire over his evening news-paper – delivered each night. It is, he tells us in martyrish tones, 'meeeee only pleasure in liiiiiife … and youse can't even lerrrrmee 'ave that!' And it's true, we can't. For Dad, reading that newspaper is true happiness. He can hold it up at his face like a barrier between us and him, then immerse himself in local crime, council business and the latest signings at Carlisle United. Dad is – he likes to tell us – a simple man with simple needs. He just wants his paper and his chair.

Dad's obsession with guarding his newspaper has become frankly delicious to me and my brother. We must not touch it before he reads it. We must not tear coupons out of it. We must not move it from the living room and read it elsewhere in the house. But with every month, as me and David grow older, we become decidedly less manageable. On one occasion my brother grabs the newspaper from the delivery boy's hands, rips the entire epistle into ten neat vertical strips and places it on the coffee table. Then we both roll around on the sofa howling at this open act of war. I can't really explain why we did this. Me and him were listening to a lot of Public Enemy at the time. Dad says nothing. He simply goes to the shops and buys another.

We are starting to call the shots.

We're not scared of him or his silences.

Dave, by the age of nearly fifteen, is around five foot ten, boy-band handsome, with Sun-In-streaked, rave-bobbed hair, an earring and a flip-top gold sovereign ring from Argos. He spends his weekends disappearing off to Legends at Warrington and coming home on Sundays with a wobbly jaw full of lies about where he slept. This club he is secretly going to sounds fantastic. Everyone is really friendly, he says. I am making plans to sneak there too. Our house is descending into small-scale anarchy. If we are grounded, we climb out of the windows and run off into the night – off to parties in student bedsits or to the pubs that will serve us. We are both on the Cumbrian truancy officer's radar; we work as a team answering the home landline when they call, pretending to be Mam or Dad and fobbing them off with excuses.

However, it is now the Night Before Christmas, so a sense of goodwill has descended; it's a time for scraping parsnips and thawing out sausage meat. Jona Lewie's 'Stop the Cavalry' is playing on the kitchen wireless. My dad's favourite Christmas song.

'*Poppa-poppa-pom-pom,*' hums my dad. '*Poppa-poppa-pom!*'

'*Poppa-pom-pom-poppa-pom!*' I sing back, bobbing along beside him.

'Wish I was at home for Chrrrrrrristmasssss!' we sing together.

Years later, this tune will start to cut me to the quick each time it resurfaces every November, floating across the ether in Westfield Stratford City's Costa Coffee, in late-night Ubers as I pass through Trafalgar Square, in Boots in Birmingham New Street Station. Festive whiplash, dragging you into a perfect memory you had no idea at the time was perfect. So cosily devastating. My grief that is not grief.

Dad found Christmas challenging. The enforced sociableness. All these folk popping by, invading his house. Unplanned. His tenseness drove my mother mad.

'And heeee's bloody walking around with a face like a slapped behind,' she'd say. 'The anti-social git ... Well, I'm letting him stew in it.'

Words like introvert, social anxiety or even Asperger's were not in our vocabulary in the North during all of my formative years. If you were in emotional pain and acting strangely, you were more likely to be told you were 'acting like a knobhead' and to 'give yourself a shake'.

But still, I knew from an early age that my father could be very insular. He especially feared the festive tap on the door. He could live without neighbours he didn't like proffering those miniature bottles of Bell's Whisky in a yuletide box that people swapped back then as goodwill gestures. He did not want to share his drum of KP nuts with Billie the Coalman or Mr Fonatana from the house on the corner. And as for all these kids in his living room, it drove him mad. All these kids, making a bloody racket.

'Your kids, George,' my mother would remind him. 'Your kids and some of their friends.'

But as 1988 was coming to a close, my dad seemed especially tricky. This may have had something to do with a gruff-sounding phone call I'd heard him having with his father in Liverpool. It was one of those phone chats I'd accidentally chanced upon by lying silently on the upstairs landing, earwigging.

Something something 'responsibilities'.

Something about doing 'the right thing'.

Something about sin.

My grandfather – or 'Parsi' as people in Liverpool called him – converted to Catholicism in the 1930s. What religion Parsi was before this was never discussed. He was brown-skinned in a sort of Middle Eastern way. Decades later I discovered that his marriage certificate gave his permanent address as a hotel close to Liverpool docks. My questions about why my Parsi was so brown went ignored. My dad had no brothers or sisters, so there were no cousins or aunties to ask either. Almost everything about my dad and his ancestors was a mystery.

When I was bolshie and demanded an answer, a collective deafness seemed to set in. But when David and I were ever taken to Liverpool as toddlers, my tiny brain could detect a sense of embarrassment.

All those awkward silences. Unsaid anger hanging in the air. Even when I won Parsi over, I could tell he was only softening towards me in spite of himself.

Parsi, like most late-life converters to Catholicism, was the most churchgoing of them all. Parsi and Nana never came for Christmas, as it was a particularly busy time of year for praying at St Kevin's in Kirkby, six miles north-east of Liverpool. Nana was five foot tall, smoked Mace Line Super Kings and was stone deaf with bad 'nerves', aside from when she was down the Mecca Bingo hall, when she could play six bingo books at once without turning a hair, hearing every number perfectly. Nana was even more religious than Parsi. By now, the shine was really starting to come off the whole God business for me. I liked the nice stories about Jesus doing good deeds, but bloody hell, church itself didn't half attract some gossips and nit-pickers. Or people flinging around words like 'sin' just to get stuff they wanted. And to top it all, there was something about Parsi's last phone call that suggested he found all of us up in Carlisle distinctly unholy.

Dad is moving a dead turkey around the house again.

He's tried resting it on top of the oven hob wrapped in tea towels, but Tadpole, one of our cats, has tried to sleep on it.

'Blooody cats, gerrrrrrawaywityer!' he shouts, swishing them off. Tadpole skedaddles for precisely three minutes before planning another attack.

Over the forty-eight hours prior to Christmas lunch, my father will move the frozen 'bird' between airing cupboards, outhouses and even the car boot in an ongoing war of attrition. After thawing, we will behold the annual gynaecological joy of watching my father retrieve a bag of giblets from the bird's rear, before going up to the elbow inside it to pack in sausage meat.

I stand in the kitchen lifting the back of my Chelsea Girl miniskirt, warming my arse on the three-bar Calor Gas fire in our kitchen. My mother's latest renovation plan – a new kitchen – has temporarily run out of money, so we only have central heating on one side of the house. We're still trying to be fancy, but the odds are always against us.

By now we have given up trying to put a Christmas tree just inside our porch, like we've seen posh people on telly do. Last year one of the local heroin addicts, in an advanced opioid state, tried to drag the tree home with him. He managed to drag the entire pot, tree and fairy lights about ten metres up the cement drive before tripping and rolling around for a bit in the wires and baubles. It was sad, but at the same time weirdly festive.

'They're giving stuff away!' Mam shouts, charging into the kitchen, back from her last-minute Christmas Eve supermarket raid. She throws twenty-four reduced-price mince pies down beside half a metre of marzipan stollen. She plonks the bags down beside my father without a hello, as they are presently only communicating via me. Maybe it's a fresh argument. Maybe it's a throwback to the ongoing tit for tat they've been having since November. Who knows?

As Mam fights to cram cartons of reduced-price brandy butter into our heaving fridge, my father pretends not to notice her arrival.

'For God's sake,' Mam huffs. 'Can you tell your father to eat something off these shelves. I need space. None of you are doing your share. Can he eat this duck pâté? It's going off.'

'Tell your mother I'm all right actually,' he says.

I turn the Calor Gas up a bar and let my bum cheeks roast through my sixty-denier tights.

'If you'd put a skirt on, we'd not need that fire,' she tuts.

'I've got a skirt on,' I snap back, thrumming the hem of my nine-inch nylon pelmet.

'You look like a street-walker,' she says.

My father busies himself with the turkey, praying for invisibility.

My mother and I are arguing constantly these days. Our rows escalate rapidly, starting with a simple request from her to bring down the six used coffee cups now growing fungus under my bed and blowing up into full-scale, door-crashing spats. We have fights where we both shout melodramatic things at high volume, for maximum effect:

'I wish you'd aborted me!'

'*Pgghghghg*, well, I wish I had too!'

'I hate you! You've never loved me!'

'Well, I hope you still feel that way when I'm DEAD!'

My mother often plays the death card, despite being in her fifties, blonde, glamorous and healthy. She knows it will shut me up rapidly as I love her. A world without her is unimaginable. Yet still the fights go on, sometimes even turning physical. Earlier this year, during a vicious row over me ruining her best saucepan while dyeing clothes, I lunged at her to grab her by the hair.

Huge mistake.

My mother is Amazonian. Unshakeable. It was like watching King Kong swat away a helicopter.

I haven't done that again.

'I mean a skirt that's actually a skirt,' she says.

'It *is* a skirt,' I huff

'Oh suit yourself,' Mam mumbles. 'Prance about with your arse out all Christmas if you like. Don't come crying to me when you spend the New Year with haemorrhoids up to your back teeth. Piles are rife in this family.'

My dad sighs deeply. It is Christmas Eve. He has three days off from work. Nowhere else to be other than within the warm bosom of his family. And if today is bad, it will only be worse when more of us arrive tomorrow.

'But it's very cold out here in the snow
Marching to and from the enemy
Oh I say it's tough, I have had enough
Can you stop the cavalry?'

Christmas Day, 1988

Every Christmas Day, Gran comes for lunch.

My mother's mother, who is also called Grace, lives on the other side of Carlisle. She arrives bearing gifts: wrapped talcum powder for Mam, a bottle of Bell's Whisky for Dad and for us kids, hard cash in brown envelopes. These offerings put a slim veneer on the fact that she thoroughly despises my father. She tries to be civil, but it is evident that Dad even wishing her 'Happy Christmas' in his sing-song Scouse twang visibly exacerbates her pernicious anaemia. Gran liked Mam's first husband perfectly well; she saw no reason to change things even if Mam was unhappy. Especially if it meant marrying a Scouse Catholic.

'Oh, she's never liked him,' Mam would say matter-of-factly if it was mentioned. I was also told that me and my dad were 'two peas in a pod', so where does that leave me?

Gran is wearing one of her good printed frocks, sort of like the ones Hattie Jacques wears in the *Carry On* films. On the lapel is a gold beetle brooch. She's tapping her walking stick to 'The Bluebell Polka' by Jimmy Shand, which my mam has put on the cassette player to please her. Beside Gran's feet sits her enormous white leather handbag – a hulking, voluminous, multi-pocketed contraption weighing at least twelve pounds. This handbag is never out of her sight. It sits on the chair by her bed when she sleeps. It contains every miscellaneous piece of paperwork needed to run her and my grandad's home:

bank statements, insurance policies, details of wills, birth certificates, plus a stack of premium bonds, or 'Ernie' as she calls them. My gran wins on the premium bonds so frequently – twenty quid here, thirty quid there – that she is affronted in the months when Ernie doesn't deliver. Her handbag also contains clippings from the *Cumberland News* of local gossip she wants to remember, a box of scented 'Thank You' notelets and several thick felt pens.

In many ways, this handbag was a rudimentary version of the Internet.

My grandmother is abrupt. Quite terrifying. She speaks as she finds. She'll cast an eye over your appearance, then root about in her handbag, produce a comb and hand it to you to tidy yourself up. She'll lambast the local mobile-shop driver about the shoddy quality of his cream crackers. She once told Jimmy Saville to unhand her at a village fête as he ambled through the crowd kissing grans.

'Well, for heaven's sake, the man stank of flesh,' she crowed. 'He's not right in the head.'

With hindsight, we probably should have listened.

Gran – Grace Senior – always carried a foldout family tree in her handbag, which she'd made herself, proving our family's lineage to the fabled Northumberland lifeboat saviour Grace Darling. As if any proof were needed that she, I or my mother – the three Graces – came from a bloodline of strident, pig-headed women who'd row a boat towards a storm against all advice. Regardless of her faults, I loved Gran madly. She could be funny as hell and when she shoved one of those brown envelopes into your hand – often behind the other grown-ups' backs – she'd do it with a little comment like, "Ere, have this, for being a bonny lass,' and you would feel completely loved.

Even on Christmas Day, Gran and Dad sitting together in a room never really felt breezy. Thankfully by the late Eighties the Dents could truly lose themselves in the feast itself. The big supermarkets had truly begun to make an impact on the festive season. We now wanted a Christmas-dinner scene like the ones we'd started seeing on TV. We would never be content with the dowdy, low-key Seventies-style Christmas meal: strictly two courses, bone-dry turkey, a couple of stingily dispersed, loveless roast spuds, boiled carrots, stewed Brussels and tinned Marrowfat peas. A gravy boat of bread sauce often lurked on the table like wallpaper paste; the grown-ups didn't seem to like it but also felt short-changed without it. On Christmas Day in the Seventies, 'afters' meant Christmas pudding. If you didn't like Christmas pudding, then you could bloody go without.

By 1988, as my gran looked at her wrist watch and waited for her dinner, in the kitchen Mam was more tense than she'd ever been before at Christmas. She was tense just like mams all over the country were now; fighting with four bubbling hobs and a full oven. Christmas Day – as a concept, a goal, a mission – had been ramped up right through December in ad breaks, on breakfast-TV cooking slots and in *News of the World* recipe pull-outs. The message was this: on Christmas Day things had to be bigger, better and perfect.

The new message wasn't just that your family should eat like better people, or posher people, on the big day. No, you should eat like *different* human beings entirely. Like shapeshifters.

Every 25 December from now on, dinner guests should be treated like the visiting Ambassador of Bolivia and his lofty retinue. Lunch should feature a starter of prawn cocktail or some sort of pâté or a soup that filled you up so you didn't really want the main course. And no more Paxo stuffing. The bird should be complemented with moist apricot and fresh herb stuffing, then served with a mountain of semolina-encrusted, duck-fat-smothered roast potatoes. Christmas pudding dislikers should be mollycoddled, cherished and presented with two or three alternatives: profiteroles, trifle or a Sara Lee yuletide log. The fruit pudding itself should be extra-special, a limited edition by a TV chef containing Cointreau and luxury peel. None of this could be eaten on your plain old dinner table using drab plates. No, Christmas dinner now needed better plates, nicer glasses and some sort of centrepiece. It may very well require a new extending dining table bought on 0 per cent finance, although I blame George Michael squarely for that. After 1984, we all wanted that dinner in Wham!'s 'Last Christmas' video, where a dozen of them all eat around a big long table, sipping fine wines, giving each other knowing glances and finishing with a snowball fight. There is no scene in that video where George explains to Pepsi & Shirlie that there's no room at the six-person dinner table, so they'll be eating their turkey on a pull-out wallpapering bench, sitting on deckchairs.

'What can I get you to drink with dinner, Grace?' my dad asks my gran, as we sit down at the table. ''Ere, Grace, little Grace, ask big Grace to get Grace something.'

With three Graces in the room, things could get very confusing.

'I'll have a glass of lemonade,' says Gran.

Gran never drank alcohol. This was no secret. If you spent more than an hour in her company, she'd manage to inform you.

'I have never touched a drop,' she'd say.

Gran was the youngest of seven girls. At the turn of the century her dad was a publican running one of the most remote, godforsaken, spit-and-sawdust inns on the hills of Catlowdy. He was a drunk, by all accounts, among other things. But the drunk part was as far as me and Mam could ever decipher. Gran never specified what her dad's other ills were, but we knew that all of her sisters – Sarah-Anne, Elsie, Francis, Jean, Nell and Beatrice – all packed a bag as soon as possible and went to Manitoba, Canada, on the strength of a small advert looking for farmhands in the back of the local gazette. Gone. None of them attempted, in any meaningful sense, to spend time with him again.

Gran stayed behind. The Second World War was her escape. She began nursing, firstly in a fever hospital and then she worked with the troops, where she met my grandad.

'Not even a small sherry?' asks my dad, semi-baiting her.

'I've never had a drop past my lips,' Gran says as I pour her a glass of pop.

'Why?' I ask, again hoping for a fuller answer.

'I've seen what it does,' she says, then she purses her lips in a way that says this line of enquiry is shut.

We're sitting around our fake pine-cone and tinsel centrepiece, using plates we only get out once a year. I have just served the starter – yes, we have a starter. It's supermarket-bought mini-smoked-salmon roulades, which I have served on chopped, undressed iceberg lettuce. It is thoroughly unlovable, but at the same time, I imagine, the type of thing Her Majesty the Queen is feasting on at Sandringham.

Gran – never one to cushion anyone's feelings – has pushed hers to the side of her plate. All this choice, all this new finickity food, left Gran aghast. For Gran, salmon came in tins; it was cooked, flaky, bony and grey around the edge. She had no time for slimy, semi-raw, smoked fish. She felt similarly about cheese. Soft cheese was unthinkable. Cheese should be orange, solid and served with crackers. You did not melt cheese. You did not buy it in a box marked Philadelphia and spread it on toast. Gran never warmed to ASDA. She didn't want twenty choices of sausage, she wanted sausage that was good. She wanted to see the man accountable for the sausage. This is why she loved the little shops. When Gran bought bacon she wanted to see the whites of the eyes of the fella who'd dismembered the pig.

'Have you heard from Liverpool this morning, George?' Gran says.

Dad's side of the family were always simply called 'Liverpool'. As if they were a scoring panel at Eurovision whom we might be going to live if the satellite link-up worked.

'Yes, I gave 'em a tinkle on the phone this morning,' my dad bats back. 'They were just off to mass, but they send their regards.'

Dad taught me that the key with small-talk is often to just give the person the answers they want to hear. He almost definitely had not called them at all.

Likewise, Gran didn't care about Liverpool. The Liverpool lot, to her mind, had several shortcomings. The main one being that they were Catholics. Gran's views on Catholics were characteristically blunt: they bred like rabbits, drank like fish and weren't to be trusted. They weren't civilised folk like us Methodists.

'Is there anymore graaaaaaaavy, precious?' my dad shouts, wearing his gold cracker crown, just as my mother's right arse cheek finally reaches her seat. The main course is much more to Gran's liking. Turkey – however one tries – defies modernisation. No matter how one titivates it. It is dry, third-rate chicken that tastes oddly like fish.

Dad's waving the half-empty gravy boat. Mam puts down her own plate, which has barely enough on it to feed a Sindy doll. She's too high on post-hob plating-up adrenaline to eat.

'Yes, there's more gravy,' she says.

Gravy is one of my mother's superpowers. Give her some sort of fatty stock, tap water and a couple of spoons of Bisto browning and she will perform alchemy.

Finally, Mam sits down with her plate. We've already begun to eat.

'All the best,' says Gran, holding up her glass of lemonade.

'Ah yes, all the best,' repeats Dad. David mutters something and clinks my glass. We are both wrestling a hangover after stealing a bottle of Warninks from the drinks' cabinet and sinking it during *Carols from Kings*.

No one says any other special Christmassy words.

No one adds a special wish or reflection. No one really looks each other directly in the eye.

For the Dents, this is verging on touchy-feely. Decades later, when I reach media London, I will spend time with families who don't eat until everyone at the table has performed a poem or given a tribute to a dead relative or performed a soliloquy from Shakespeare. I will always feel awkward, if not a little irate, around such naked show-offy emotion. We show our love in my family in smaller ways.

'Good gravy, Grace,' my dad says to my mam.

'Yes, grand gravy, Grace,' agrees Gran.

Once the Christmas pudding has been microwaved in its plastic bowl and served with custard, there is a sense that Christmas has now peaked. A curiously post-coital sense of silliness sets in. What was all that about? All those weeks of rushing, plotting and panicking; who was the ritual for? For each other? For Jesus? Why do we bother with all this fuss? Yet here I am, writing this as a grown woman, knowing that while I have breath in my body, I will strive to make every Dent Christmas more or less exactly the same.

Gran and Dad retreat to the living room where they sit side by side, gobs open, snoring through James Bond, which is inexplicably playing at ninety-eight decibels.

Mam and me clear the table, sorting leftovers into piles for a turkey curry and bubble and squeak. A tap on the dining-room window heralds my mam's best friend, Gail. She's wearing her best Marshall Ward's catalogue frock and bearing gifts: a packet of Embassy Reds, a bottle of Bacardi and some amazing tittle-tattle about other folks' Christmas dinners.

'Well,' Gail says, gathering steam, 'Heather's lot aren't even sitting down until five! She's not even got her carrots peeled! They're busy playing with the Scalextric.'

'Well, five o'clock is too late,' tuts my mother. 'They'll not want any teas later.'

''Ere, did I tell you her and Frank aren't having turkey this year? They're having roast topside of beef. He reckons he doesn't like turkey!'

'Well, that's just peculiar, if you ask me,' says my mother.

'Well, he *IS* peculiar,' says Gail.

I love earwigging on Mam and her friends. And on Gran when she's in full flow. It's around now that I'm starting to scribble things down in jotters. Not just the things I want to remember, but the exact way it was actually said. I love the Cumbrian dialect and sing-song rhythm of the words. I love the mesh of titbits about local life; whose bloke's done a runner, who's as 'fat as butter', who's a pisshead, who's up the duff and who's a lazy slattern who never washes her sheets.

'Well, her youngest, Marcus, had a bust-up face from Black-eye Friday,' Gail says. 'Got clouted by one of the bouncers outside Cat's Whiskers.' Black-eye Friday is the last Friday before Christmas in Carlisle when the majority of factories and offices finish early and the workforce hit the pubs and clubs and get sloshed. The ensuing annual carnage – involving many fights – has been given its own unofficial nickname.

Cat's Whiskers nightclub on Black-eye Friday was not for the meek.

'Terrible,' tuts Mam. 'What a way to be carrying on!'

I bring Gail an ashtray. She mixes me a small, potent Bacardi and Pepsi, and slyly hands me an Embassy Red that I stuff quickly between my boobs to smoke later.

I return to the kitchen, where I start stacking our fancy dishwasher. Obviously, I'm rinsing each plate under the tap first as it's the Eighties and none of us trust this machine entirely. I'm listening to the Colorblind James Experience on John Peel's Festive 50, which I've taped off Radio 1, as I stoop to fill the bottom shelf with dinner plates.

'… well, he's been in a right mard for weeks anyway,' I overhear Mam say.

'He's been in a mard since you set eyes on him in 1971,' Gail says. 'How can you tell the difference?'

They both laugh.

I put the forks and knives standing upright in the holder and take a large slurp of delicious, sweet Bacardi.

They're talking about Dad and his moodiness, although we all know it really isn't that funny.

And then Gail draws on a ciggie, exhales and says: 'So has he had any more word from the girls? After that first letter?'

'Not that I know of,' Mam says. 'Not since the one I saw. I can't make head nor tail of him, though. He's very subdued.'

And then they remember that I'm next door in the kitchen and change the subject.

I knock back the rest of the Bacardi.

Who are these girls who have written my dad a letter?

1990

In the second-floor café in Binns Department Store in Carlisle, I'm sat with my friends Darren (Carlisle's biggest Smiths fan) and Caroline (with blonde hair and all the petticoats), making a lukewarm hot chocolate with squirty cream last almost two and a half hours. Binns is the most glamorous store in Cumbria. It has an Estée Lauder concession and a homeware section where you can buy a Denby Pottery gravy boat or a Moulinex potato ricer. On the second floor, follow the whiff of chips and there is a restaurant where mams and aunties come to rest their feet mid-shop and eat scones and jam. Although annoyingly for customers and staff, the best tables near the window are perpetually commandeered by us: a band of teenage goths, hippies, fledgling ravers, Morrissey devotees, Stone Roses boys and the occasional off-duty soccer hooligan who reckons himself a hardman but secretly loves talking about Pink Floyd with the pretty indie girls.

Every town and city up and down the United Kingdom had a café like this in the Eighties; a place teens had taken to their heart. But while the Binns café was pivotal to our social lives, we in turn were disastrous for its profits.

I was its worst sort of regular customer, making a hot chocolate last as long as a three-course meal before inevitably stealing the cup. In my bedroom at home I had a growing haul of thieved Binns saucers, plates and ashtrays.

'So how does it feel,' Darren says, 'to set yourself up as our very own Oscar Wilde?'

'Oh shurrup,' I say, a bit distracted.

I am not really myself.

As I lick cream off the teaspoon and push it into my handbag, Darren is teasing me about my second appearance in the *NME* letters page. Swells has chosen me for print again, this time defending The Cure's Robert Smith. OK, not the whole letter this time, more a snippet. As I'd affixed a stamp to the envelope and pushed it into the post box, I knew even then it wasn't one of the best things I'd written.

But I've had other things on my mind.

I cannot claim that the news that my father has two other daughters has come as a complete shock.

Shocked isn't the word. Even if the way I found out was quite shocking.

This morning, Saturday, at around six, my dad walked into my bedroom when I was half asleep. He leaned into the bed, kissed my head and said, 'All right, precious, I dunno if Mam's told you what's going on, but I need to go and see Jackie and Tina.'

He kissed me again on the forehead, then got into his van and drove off down the M6 motorway to Liverpool to make amends with his other kids. The ones he left behind in the Sixties.

I sat up in bed and rubbed sleep from my eyes.

I definitely did not cry. Or go and find my mam.

I sat in bed for a few hours watching *The Chart Show* on ITV, hoping for a rewind on the Happy Mondays on the indie chart. Teenagers in the Eighties were very outwardly undramatic. We'd not been primed yet by a steady diet of American TV drama and reality shows to emit neat soundbites about our feelings. We did not expect hugs when we left or entered rooms, let alone feel that our issues needed to be heard or seen.

And as I say: this news was shocking but not entirely a shock.

After all, during my attempt to win the Brownie matchbox game seven years before, I'd found that black-and-white photo while rifling through my father's bedside drawer.

I shouldn't have been in that drawer anyway.

I wasn't supposed to rifle in drawers.

The photo was of two girls, standing by a countryside gate on a ramblers' path. Smiling. On a day out. Just like the sort of days out my family went on, if Mam could ever prise Dad out of his chair.

I'd stared at that photo for a long time.

I did not know those little girls.

They could, I'd tried to reason, be the Canadian side of our family. But Dad had no affection whatsoever for Mam's relatives. For a tiny family, we were certainly a pile of divisions.

Maybe, I'd thought, they were kids that belonged to one of Dad's army friends and he'd kept them just to be polite. They didn't mean anything.

I'd puzzled over the two girls' faces for a minute or so, and then put the photo back in the drawer. Then I'd pretended I'd not seen it. Children's minds are slippery, pragmatic things. We come fresh from the box, hellbent on self-preservation. Dad's other kids were always there in a sense; they were a puzzle for me to solve. But being small and distracted by the magic of Noel Edmonds' *Multi-Coloured Swap Shop* or a bag of pink sugar prawns, or Adam Ant and Diana Dors doing the 'Prince Charming' dance, it took me a few years to focus properly.

And then the phone calls from Parsi to Dad had begun. I now realise he had been acting as a go-between.

I thought about the clues that had led me here. Dad's daughters had been there in a thousand awkward silences whenever I'd asked about the past. They were there in bitten lips and half-overheard adult mutterings. They were there in the faces of my Catholic Scouse grandparents, who, being against divorce, treated us kids like an unpleasant smell.

They were there in my dad's embrace when sometimes, out of nowhere, he'd seem taken by emotion and would drag my tiny face against his rough soldier stubble and say, 'Oh come here, precious, you're my only little girl.'

Which I realised now actually meant: 'The only little girl I have left, because I have mislaid not one, but two others to date.'

As I sat on the edge of the bed, counting out coins for the 68 bus up town, I already felt slightly sorry for my dad. I was already making excuses.

Over the coming years, whenever I would talk of my dad's life, people would reply with their own family skeletons, and then they'd bring me their own excuses too. They'd tell me of double lives or mams who disappeared overnight. And of grandads who left to fight in wars and forgot to go home, then got married again bigamously to prettier, younger women in warmer countries. They'd tell me of babies left on church doorsteps, or small children signed over to council care, with the original parents shuffling away without a trace. My dad's charade in the Sixties was not a highly unusual state of affairs. In the 'good old days' people would, could and *did* just disappear. It's less painful for us if we cling to the idea that our elders did these things for reasons that went with the era: out of shame or because of religion or poverty or some other very difficult set of circumstances. We don't want to think it was down to pure selfishness. Or that sometimes, in the 'good old days', people were just absolute arseholes.

* * *

In the Binns café, interrupted by the arrival of the occasional toasted teacake, we're discussing Johnny Marr from The Smiths making electronic music with Barney from New Order. It still seems weird to us, but it's what lots of indie folk are doing now, making music full of bleeps and synths and stuff you can dance to. Some of my indie-worshipping friends are making excursions to a club in Manchester called The Haçienda, which is dead hard to get into but once inside I hear it's like some sort of Shangri-La where everyone is friendly and no one drinks alcohol. This intrigues me.

Talking about music and telly and popstars and making my friends laugh with my thoughts is when I come alive. Almost all other times I feel swivel-eyed with teenage hormones. Carlisle is small and claustrophobic and full of people who care how you look and dress, and I'm sick to the back teeth of worrying what 'they' think. Whoever they are. They, according to all of our mams, are a shadowy group of ever-observant souls who are perpetually on the edge of 'having a field day' about the length of our skirts or our haircuts. Over the past twelve months I have been going on the train by myself to London to see Bob. I sit for seven hours, ten minutes – in the smoking carriage, where all the best people sit – to spend time with him and his girlfriend, Vron. They're both twenty-five and squatting in Manor House. Mam agrees to this as I am supposed to be sightseeing – Nelson's Column, the Houses of Parliament and so on – but instead, aged fifteen, I just tag along with their London life. We go to the Sir George Robey pub in Seven Sisters for a night called ClubDog, where they play Iggy Pop and The Cult, and to The Catacombs in Manor House. We go to Heaven on a Saturday with Bob and Vron's gay friends and eat food on Sundays in Hare Krishna cafés. I become accustomed to being woken by their pets – liberated laboratory rats – nibbling my feet.

During this time Bob has kept a tactful silence about his stepdad, although he admits he once met the little girls in the photos. He buys a broadsheet newspaper called the *Guardian*. It's not like anything I've ever read in our house before. I love to read the *Weekend* magazine, where a woman called Julie Burchill with big hair has the front-page column every week to write about almost anything: her love life, the Gaza Strip, the royal family. Then, the following week, the letters page is chock full of people absolutely pigging furious at her. Or – and this happens too – they're madly in love with her. No half measures. She is a name that provokes a reaction. She is seen by everyone and she is making an impact. I want to make an impact like this too. I entirely gloss over how it must feel to be hated and focus on how it must feel to be so loved. I love this idea of being so loved. Being loved like this must be like the gates of heaven flying open and being constantly bathed in a celestial shimmer. How can you possibly feel pain, or sadness, or that your dad is completely not the person he pretended to be for the whole of your childhood, when you walk into a room and they all know your name?

But I have absolutely no idea how. I want to make people feel how I felt when I saw Kim Deal from the Pixies walk onstage in Preston and play the bassline to 'Debaser'. I want to wind people up like La Cicciolina, with her flower crown, pink diamanté gown and one nipple bared, setting Italian politics alight. I'd settle for changing the atmosphere in the room like my Aunty Frieda, who married a posh man and now causes chaos whenever she appears. I mean, who the hell does Aunt Frieda think she is?! I want to be like Magenta Devine who presents *Network 7* and especially Paula Yates off *The Tube*. Paula had all of Duran Duran and David Bowie at her wedding, holding her aloft in her deep-red dress in one of the photos. Sadly, I do not resemble Paula or Magenta or La Cicciolina. I am a short teenager from the arse-end of Cumbria – not even the Lake District part, the inner-city part where the heroin addicts live. I have weird teeth, a growingly huge arse from eating ASDA 'Whoops!' reduced cookies and an accent that sounds like an angry cormorant on Morecambe pier swooping to steal chips.

But I have had one and a quarter letters printed in the *NME*, and that is a start.

When Dad got home that evening, he was subdued. Mam gave him his tea on a tray. He did not wish to talk about any of this daughters business when asked. There was certainly no apology to me.

'Hang on, I thought you knew,' Mam said when I tackled her on the subject.

'No, I didn't know,' I said.

'Oh right, I thought you did,' she said. 'You had your nose in everything as a kid.'

'Does David know?' I said.

'He must do by now,' said my mam. 'He'll have overheard what's going on.'

I still loved my dad, and the excuses I was making for him were getting more water-tight by the minute. None of this could be my dad's fault. These terrible things could not possibly be his doing. Leaving an ex-wife and two children – I bet he didn't want those things in the first place. She probably trapped him. Yes, the more I thought about it, my dad had almost certainly been tricked.

CHAPTER 3

Pickled Egg

1982

'Always begin at the outside and move inwards,' she says, pointing to the extra knives and forks. 'And after a few glasses of wine, no one cares what you do anyway.'

Aunt Frieda is so incredibly glamorous.

At a family function, aged almost nine years old, I find myself sat close to her. It is Gran's birthday and we are going somewhere far too posh for the likes of us. The fuss about what we should wear and how we will all get there has gone on for weeks. Twelve of us are eating in a function room beside an auction mart in West Cumbria, which does something slightly above pub meals.

Frieda, a distant relative on Mam's side, arrives wearing a chunky gold bracelet with her name on. Whispers at the table price it at over £200.

From the very limited set menu, she chooses the Florida Cocktail starter with bitter pieces of grapefruit and pink Thousand Island dressing, while everyone else sticks safely to cock-a-leekie soup. Then she orders fish on the bone with its head still attached.

Back then, the story of Aunt Frieda was told to me as a terrible warning.

In the Fifties, Aunty Frieda played the fiddle. A large man-sized fiddle set against her tiny booby frame, offset by a shock of honey-blonde, Cumbrian-farming-stock hair and a smattering of pale-brown freckles. She played 'The Bluebell Polka'. She played 'Scotland the Brave'. She played 'D'ye Ken John Peel?' and all the other tunes that got a Cumberland party started in 1955. She played 'When Irish Eyes Are Smiling', flanked by a band of burly men with flyaway, badger-like eyebrows and tweed trousers that smelled of piss and ale even after being sponged down and hung to dry night after night in damp outhouses. They accompanied her on the accordion and tin whistle. She played at pie-and-pea suppers in dusty village halls from Caldbeck to Gretna – gatherings where farm folk pedalled miles on pushbikes and for a shilling they'd get some music and a slab of pie filled with oxtail or cheap stewing steak, wrapped in homemade shortcrust made with suet, all gleaned from cows who'd chewed the cud within two miles of the hall. Pie, with a ladle of fat, soft peas and a thick beef gravy made from blood, fat and bones. It was a chance to sit down, escape the farm for a few hours and have 'sech a gran' craic', as Cumberland folk would say.

My Aunty Frieda played the fiddle at beetle-drive evenings where local women with tight mouths and twenty-four-hour girdles played cards and politely took cash off each other, sweeping their vast bosoms westwards and discussing lesser women's errant husbands. She played at point-to-points where farmers raced their horses. She played hunt balls where landowners and local minor aristocrats gathered to chase a fox and rip its tiny frame from nose to snout into a pile of entrails – for fun – then drink whisky and eat pork pies. And then the band would play. Everyone the next day always remembered Frieda: full of confidence, spark and music.

Obviously, a lot of people found all this confidence and spark infuriating. They liked the music, but it came with a lot of sheer brass neck. That said, if they thought about it – which they did a lot, because there was nothing else to do in Fifties Cumberland – Frieda wasn't breaking any laws. It wasn't against the law to be confident. In time, Frieda began to play her fiddle at society weddings, which meant she occasionally stayed out late, past midnight, sometimes until dawn. She drank gilt-rimmed coupes of brandy with Babysham and began to mingle with people far above her station. She met doctors and factory owners and even the local lord. She met people the likes of whom my family only ever saw by appointment, or if they were up before the court. Folk we'd never dream of just striking up a chat with, let alone biting back at with a punchline. 'She carries on like she's one of them,' people said. 'Like she thinks she's supposed to be there,' people said. 'She thinks she's it, she does.'

Frieda was as good at talking as she was luring people to dance the Eightsome Reel. When a job came up as a part-time secretary at Barley Grange Hall, up at the big house, to work for a local toff called Lord Eric helping with his correspondence, well, off she trotted. In her good skirt and her mother's good blouse, she went up the long gravel drive, where no one common ever went other than to clean the floors or perhaps take a chance to sell tea towels. 'Well, she wasn't there long before she was taking down more than *notes*,' people at the beetle drive said, their lips as tight as a cold cat's anus.

Lord Eric – divorced once, twenty-five years older – found Frieda indispensable. Soon she was driving about with him in his Aston Martin with a headscarf on. Her accent became clipped and her vowels flatter, and if you had no idea of where she'd come from she could pass as posh. 'She isn't just talking like the Queen,' women crowed at gin rummy nights, 'I think the Queen these days models herself on Frieda.' Every syllable of their envy was audible. The sound of their cards being chopped and dealt echoed around the chilly village hall now that Frieda didn't have time to play the fiddle for them anymore.

Eventually Aunt Frieda married Eric and that is how she got her title. Lady Frieda. An actual *title*. Her use of which lasted much longer than their mutual love. That liaison burned bright and fast until it became icy and belligerent, although the details of the eventual split gave the locals even more entertainment. Regardless, being a Lady, which she still was, was terribly useful. People's faces shifted when she walked into a room. I loved it. The way the energy changed.

The low-level pandemonium she caused at wakes and wedding receptions. There was always a table in any restaurant for her when she telephoned.

This was all meant to be a terrible portent.

That racehorse she invested in with her plentiful divorce settlement and spent weekends watching from a box at the side of tracks? Money down the drain. Those handsome younger men she romanced? They were just using her for her money. The time she toured South Africa in a campervan? She was living like a *gypsy*, basically. None of this sounded bad to me. It sounded absolutely bloody brilliant. On our flickering Grundig telly, I saw the inside of five-star hotels on a travel programme called *Whicker's World*. I saw Manhattan through the eyes of Clive James. I saw Keith Floyd in France eating truffle and foie gras and caviar on blinis with Krug champagne. In Jackie Collins novels the heroine flew on first-class flights where you turned left at the top of the stairs, drank Gran Marnier at 38,000 feet and, if you were lucky, got titted up by the pilot. I saw pictures of Princess Margaret in Antigua and I thought, well, that seems *much* nicer than Currock. Sometimes folk from Carlisle went on coach trips to London. Proper fancy it was; you spent two days in a B&B in Bayswater, which included a trip to Madame Tussauds and Knightsbridge. They'd come home clutching their prized Harrods shopper bag and use it to bring back spuds from Walter Willson's supermarket.

This status symbol proved you'd been brave enough to walk through the doors.

'They check your shoes and what you look like on the way in,' Margaret at Number 17 told us, whisking by with her crumpled green shopper. 'They weren't going to let our Kenneth in, as he had a hole in his moccasins.'

When I get there, I thought, Harrods will be the very first place I go.

Something that is very misunderstood about some of the working classes is that, given the flicker of a chance, we will become the greatest dandies of all. The showiest of show-offs. The grandest eccentrics. We'll have the biggest gobs and the hardest nerves. With the most imperceptible beckoning, we will pirouette from the thirty-watt-bulb glow of our MDF-divided box bedrooms and behave in the most obstreperous, albeit charming, manner. As if we had not *just as much* of a right but *more* of a right than privileged folk. And once we're in, you can't get us out. The day after that posh birthday meal, I sat in the fields in Currock by the railway track, by the gypsy horses, eating a pickled egg out of a paper bag. I did not know how I could possibly get from one place to the other, but I knew that one day, like Aunt Frieda, I wanted to walk into restaurants and feel the invisible chaos I'd caused. And when I did, I would do it with my shoulders back, and my chin tilted upwards, and a swish in my step. And I would con everyone completely that here, yes, exactly *here*, was where I was supposed to be.

1990

In 1990, I styled out imposter syndrome heading into sixth-form block in a MK One batwing jumper and a pair of bold fractal leggings, which were unforgiving on my tree-trunk thighs. Sixth form took place in a few classrooms with their own stairwell at the side of the school. In the common room a manky third-hand sofa spewed its innards onto the floor and a large graffitied Aciiiid House smiley face beamed on the wall. The place stank of Loulou by Cacherel, Insignia shower gel, damp trainers and Options Choc-o-Orange sachets. On day two of the new term someone who will remain nameless put magic mushrooms in the communal kettle and I had to go home early as I was getting tracers trying to look at the blackboard. As 'young adults' we were now allowed to ditch our uniforms, wear as much make-up as we desired and express our own personal styles. The results, in my case, were perpetually woeful. The Nineties were not a vintage time for everyday girls who bought their fanciest clothes from the local C&A or market stall and their make-up from a cut-price shop called Cosmicuts at the top of Botchergate. A lot of Eighties and Nineties make-up did more to hinder than help. Foundation came in three colours: anaemia white, ripe peach or terracotta. If you were a woman of colour in the United Kingdom in the Nineties, well, God help you. You had to get your stuff by sending a postal order to an advert in the back of *Woman* magazine and choosing shade one, two or three.

And if you were pockmarked, sallow, bumpy or had pores like a sieve, well, hard cheese, because primer wasn't invented. Furthermore, Nineties lipsticks always bled after about ten minutes, all sheer lip shades seemed to contain cheap glitter and most dark red shades often came out blue once you got them home. Most of the time I looked atrocious. But then we all did.

No mortal woman knew how to apply blusher correctly. We splodged it roughly over 'the apples of our cheeks' so that our faces slid downwards like Salvador Dalí clocks. Eyeliner was still only really on the shelves in the form of cheap kohl pencils that were too scratchy to apply to your eyelid and cracked every time you tried to sharpen them. I used to shove this kohl on my watery eye rims to look like Béatrice Dalle in *Betty Blue* but instead looked like Beetlejuice.

'Your eyes look like pissholes in the snow,' Mam would say helpfully as I ambled out of the door.

'Thank you,' I'd say.

'And your lips look like a corpse,' she'd add.

'It's Heather Shimmer actually,' I'd grump. 'What do you know about looking nice? You're, like, fifty-four years old. You're an old-age pensioner.'

Being fifty-four felt like an actual crime. How dare she try to tell me anything? She had a point about the eyeliner, though. And the foundation tide marks and the split ends from backcombing my hair too much. God knows how any of us found each other sexy. All early-Nineties sex was fuelled mainly by Thunderbird, peach Lambrini blush and low standards. I didn't know a woman who wouldn't have given Kurt Cobain one, and he looked like a poorly stuffed scarecrow.

Sixth form was also the beginnings of my lifelong battle to be slinky. After a few relatively carefree years of snacking on reduced-price double-chocolate muffins for breakfast, there was a price to pay. By the age of sixteen I was noticing how easily fat would settle on my hips, bottom and stomach.

'Oh, you're like me and your gran – big hips,' Mam would say with some level of glee.

Obviously, I could take it off again just as quickly. I'd just starve for a bit and go to bed hungry. I'd smoke half a packet of Consulate menthol a day and drink a lot of Diet Coke. Or just eat the exact same food as before, but drier. Because what we knew for sure in the Eighties and Nineties was that fat, oil and butter were the actual problems.

'You can eat as many chip butties as you like,' Alison Bright would say as we puzzled over our French pluperfect verbs, 'as long as it's oven chips and no Golden Churn on your bread or 'owt!'

At this age, me and most of my female friends became masters of calorie counting. Our minds hoovered up and stored for life every approximate kcal per hundred-gram portion. Few Generation X women can look at a plate of food and not make a rough guess of how much it eats into a 1,200-calorie-per-day target. These things would be there in my mind, lurking forever. The fewer calories you consumed a day, the better. One thousand calories per day was being good.

'It's sixty-five calories a tin,' my slim, gorgeous friend Sonia would tell me as we dawdled to the school bus. She is extolling the wonders of Weight Watchers' Mediterranean tomato soup. 'You can have it with two dry Ryvita, and that's your dinner. My mam did it for six weeks and she could wear a cossie in Menorca!' The can was as big as your palm. It was opaque red seepage with an occasional decadent fleck of tomato skin. It tasted of vinegary ditch water. The dry Ryvitas stuck in my throat and then I couldn't sleep at night as my stomach growled while I dreamt of morning when I could have three tablespoons of Special K with skimmed milk.

Yes, I knew 800 calories a day was too low and might make me feel faint, but fuck it, by Saturday I could wear a catsuit to The Haçienda and dance to Todd Terry and I would look fucking incredible again, for a bit.

I took English, history and French at A level. They felt like the kinds of subjects someone arty might take. And now, with all the illiterate kids and the pyromaniacs gone, there was a chance to get down to some actual learning. Unfortunately, Shakespeare's *Henry IV, Part 1* and sixteenth-century European history were hard-pressed to be as compelling as the fantastic-quality MDMA that was freely available across north-west England during the early Nineties.

'We're going to Leeds tonight,' I'd announce to my mother at Saturday teatime, breezing through the living room in a second-hand crushed-velvet Lady Miss Kier trouser suit that smelled of mothballs with three doves stashed under my right tit. My father would immediately stand up from his chair under the pretense of remembering a light bulb that needed changing. He now had one daughter who was a pseudo intellectual sixth-form crackpot who was either fighting her mother or going to shady parties, another daughter in Liverpool who sort of but not quite forgave him for his twenty-year absence and wanted to be in touch and a third who had met him again, thought some more and then realised that she didn't forgive him at all. He wasn't having much luck with women.

'Leeds?' Mam'd say.

'Leeds,' I'd say.

'That's about a hundred miles away!' she'd explode.

'Yeah ... it's a party,' I'd mutter.

'In a house?' she'd say.

'No ... just a thing. In a warehouse where you dance,' I'd say, hoping she hadn't read any of the tabloid newspaper reports on this type of thing too closely.

'Will there be any food?' screams my mother.

'Yes, *there's a bloody buffet*,' I'd say.

'Well, I hope you eat some of it,' she'd say, 'and not just booze.'

I wouldn't be boozing.

And I wouldn't be hungry at all.

I often wonder what happened to the millions of people I met during these years. That whole generation of wasters double dropping in the queue, then staggering about with their eyes rolling back in their skulls like boiled eggs escaping from their faces. All those Sunday mornings lost in strange houses, dancing in people's attics, in barns and back houses, walking home from parties across fields with no shoes on. Where are they all now?

None of these things helped my route into academia. I may have written some terrible sixth-form poetry along the way (though like all poetry written as a teen, it should be put into a shredder and the remnants burned with petrol to spare everyone's blushes), but as for actual studying, the problem was A levels need an eye for detail, and Mondays after a Saturday night were at best hazy and Tuesdays were just difficult. On Wednesdays I'd stare under duress at my A-level notes on the fourteenth-century peripatetic courts of Castile and Aragon. By Thursday we'd make plans, merge funds and then party at the Sub Club or The Arches in Glasgow. We'd brazen the queue for The Haçienda in Manchester or dance till three at the Arena at Middlesbrough, then travel home in the back of someone's Ford Escort van.

I'd love to blame Dad and his errant ways for all of this. But I've never been able to blame anyone else for my behaviour with a straight face. Blaming your dad for the idiotic stuff you do – in youth, as well as beyond – is very middle class.

CHAPTER 4

Never Mind the Tunnock's

October 1992

'So that blue tattoo on his arm, the one he covers up,' I say to Mam, 'is that his first wife's name?' I'm packing a suitcase and detaching a poster of Michael Hutchence with his big doe love-me eyes from my wall, leaving Blu Tack scars behind.

I am leaving home. Mam looks sad, but sad in a way that leaves room to start knocking down the MDF that separates my bedroom and the bathroom, and installing a mock neo-palatial sunken bath with a two-speed whirlpool.

'What?' she says. 'Oh, that? That blurry tattoo? It says "Vera". He used to scrub at his arm with iron wool to make it blurry. That's how they got rid of tattoos then.'

It's October. I've just turned nineteen. Six weeks ago, clutching two Bs that I'd somehow scraped despite everything, I spent ten minutes on the telephone with a kind woman in a university administration office far away in Scotland. That call changed the entire course of my life. I got into uni on 'clearing'. After some garbled chat about who I was and my love of words, whoever this brilliant, understanding human

101

being was took pity on me and shoved me in to study a BA in English literature. I had a place at the University of Stirling. No, I didn't know where it was either. Nevertheless, I said yes on the spot. I got my dad's big AA map down and found it. Stirling was on a mountain in the middle of nowhere, between Glasgow and Edinburgh. Dad said he'd drive me there.

Two days later a reading list arrived via Royal Mail, with a cover note, which I carried around with me for years, that said, 'Good luck, Miss Dent.' The list was ten books long, consisting of Iain Banks's *The Wasp Factory* and *Bonfire of the Vanities* by Tom Wolfe and *The Island of Dr Moreau* by H.G. Wells. I didn't know how I was going to shoplift all of them, but I could make a start that day. I'd slid downwards for a while on the game of snakes and ladders, but I was on the rise again. If I studied English and maybe worked for the student paper – wasn't that what famous people did? They edited student papers or maybe performed in plays and then they were noticed by BBC Two and got their own series, were catapulted into the nation's hearts and spent weekends hanging around the Groucho Club drinking White Russians with Sigue Sigue Sputnik.

'How long was he married to Vera?' I say to Mam, taking down a poster of Matt Dillon brooding in a vest.

Mam's face creases to think.

'Oh, no, he wasn't married to Vera, he was married to Maureen,' she says.

'You said Vera,' I correct her. 'On his arm, Vera.'

'Oh, Vera was the one he was with before he went in the army,' says Mam.

'I've never heard of her,' I say.

'Yes, you have,' she says. 'That's the one he had the little boy with.'

'He had the what?' I say, feeling the colour drain from my face.

'Michael,' she says. 'Oh.'

I look at her.

'I thought you knew about this one,' she says.

'No, I didn't know about this one,' I say, the floor moving beneath me.

My father, I had just found out, also had a son called Michael. Somewhere, out there. As far as Mam knew, he was not in touch with him.

My father, it transpired, did not join the army as a teenager out of a post-war patriotic fervour; the line he'd spun my entire life. Dad was a military man! All he'd yearned to do from being a tiny boy was to join up and be prepared to fight for his country in case the Nazis made another appearance! This was a lie too. He just got someone in Liverpool up the duff and was basically on the bloody run. I wasn't angry at Dad. It's hard to stay angry at a person when your only chance of freedom requires them to give you cash for your first month's rent.

I never, ever spoke to Dad about Michael. He made talking about things he didn't want to talk about impossible. But I did think over the years that it must have been very difficult for Dad getting someone pregnant early in the Fifties when he had such Catholic parents. My ability to find excuses for my dad was pretty honed by this point: Michael was all religion's fault. If anything, this mess-up was on the Pope. And the telephone exchange. I mean, how was Dad supposed to stay in touch with his first child when he was in the army, right?

I wandered out onto the tarmac outside Southdale Street, smoked a menthol Silk Cut and rubbed Cilla's belly as she kipped with four paws in the air, under the 'Warning – Dog' sign. I loved Currock – shaking the Currock part out of me was going to prove very hard – but it was time for me to go.

In Scotland I was introduced to the perilous joys of Buckfast Tonic Wine.

'It's made in an abbey by wee monks,' my flatmate Agnes told me, pouring me a glass in my first week as a Stirling resident. This fortified caffeinated grape juice had quite the reputation, although not quite as holy water; rather for encouraging drinkers to roll about in the streets and fight the local police. If you overlooked all that, it was actually rather drinkable. For the mornings after, I was tutored in the restorative power of a can of cold Barr's Irn-Bru: a bright-orange, bubblegum-flavoured, hangover-blitzing nectar. It was 'made in Scotland from girders' according to the adverts that played on Grampian TV. I found the adverts intoxicating. I'd grown up eight miles from the Scottish border in the blissfully ignorant belief that if you ever strayed over there they probably ate and drank the same things we did.

I was wrong. Every day in my new adopted country was a fresh treat. In my first year I learned to love the claggy happiness of Tunnock's caramel wafers wrapped in fawn tartan wrappers. These delicious things required serious commitment to chomp through. Any English fairy could eat a Penguin or a Breakaway. Only Scotland could invent a chocolate biscuit that actually hurts your mouth. They are a nation of glorious contrarians. They take something perfectly design-friendly, like a sausage, call it Lorne Sausage and serve it in regimented flat rectangles. They didn't bother with fancy modern sliced bread like Mighty White; no, their sliced bread looked like something from 1940. It was a thin, tall loaf, wrapped in tartan-patterned greaseproof paper. At breakfast they added white tatty scones to their fry-ups – mashed left-over spud mixed with flour, cut into triangles and fried in a pan full of leftover bacon fat. Each Sunday night, my flat-mates would return from visits to their families with 'tablet' – a sort of homemade fudge made from condensed milk and sugar. Everyone's 'wee nan' had a secret recipe.

None of the above did much for the size of my arse, because, roughly speaking, none of the real joys of Nineties Scottish cuisine were terribly healthy. Although I never set eyes on a battered Mars Bar – a tourist thing newspapers harped on about in the Nineties – it does give away something really, really brilliant about Scotland. They took chip shops very seriously; much more so than the English. In Stirling, the fryers were on from 11 a.m. till 11 p.m. daily, seven days a week. Chips were fresh, hot and fried in beef dripping, then pelted with salt and sweet brown sauce. Any item within reason was flung into the deep-fat fryer: slices of pizza, pakoras, onion rings, haggis, white puddings, black puddings, sausages and chicken tikka. The Scots, I found out quickly, had their own specific chip-shop language. Any item with chips was 'a supper', even if you were eating it at 11 a.m. Anything without chips was 'single', almost as if you were explaining its relationship status. The Scots – confirming that they are God's own people – invented something called 'the munchy box': a fourteen-inch pizza box containing a sumptuous smorgasbord of pick 'n' mix deep-fried things: onion bhajis, battered sausages, shaved kebab meat, chicken nuggets, scampi and so on and so forth. The munchy box was a positive boon during the Nineties for stoned people playing *Mortal Kombat* on Super Nintendo who could only eat with one hand while leading Sonya through martial arts battles.

Dad drove me to Stirling in a van brim full of all my worldly belongings. Other Freshers seemed to be travelling light, arriving with a small rucksack containing *The Dark Side of the Moon* on cassette and some wet wipes to tide them over until they next went *home*. But as I made this leap from one world to another, I was sure that was the last time I'd live in Cumbria again. I arrived with my beloved fake Eames chair that made me look like one of the intellectuals on Channel 4's cool anarchic debate show *After Dark*. I packed my stereo, my Deee-Lite CDs, my DJ Sasha bootleg cassettes and several split-leg dresses and feather boas, in case an emergency Brand New Heavies concert broke out. As the Nineties continued, my fashion sense did not improve.

'Why are ye' wanderin' aboot like a pure bam?' Agnes would say, when I appeared in the kitchen in a charity-shop cocktail dress that made me look, I supposed, exactly like Jackie Onassis.

'You're wearing a Rangers tracksuit,' I'd snap back, putting on my oversized sunglasses. 'You have no right to talk about fashion.'

Agnes played football for Stirling Women and in the holidays, aged nineteen, ran one of the bars at Ibrox Stadium.

'Seriously, mon, get te' fuck,' she'd laugh. 'I'm casual. You're chippin' aboot lookin' like a bluebottle.'

As a settler from another country, I was always treated kindly by the Scots, despite the fact that thirty years of Tory government had left millions of them even more resentful about 'the fuckin' English' than ever before. Many felt forgotten, looked down upon, swindled and snubbed all at once. The dream of Scottish independence never felt far from the surface in any pub chat. Cos they 'hated the fuckin' English, maan'. All of us.

'The thing is, youse are all a bunch of posh yah-yah cunts, that's why,' my friend Gary would say in thick Kilmarnock tones.

'What, even me?' I'd say.

He'd cave immediately.

'Actually ... no, not the Northerners,' he'd say. 'Youse lot are OK. Youse lot are like us.'

Something has been vaguely troubling me about Dad, which happened on the very first day of term. It was a very subtle thing, but I dwelt on it for weeks afterwards.

'This is Grace,' my father shouts across the car park in a weird American accent. 'You'll be seeing a lot of her.'

A group of bewildered Finnish PhD students, returning for their final year at university, turn around to stare at me. I'm an anonymous Fresher they have no reason to know, unloading a car. They shrug and walk away. I never see those students ever again. Or any of the other strangers my father insists on introducing me to on my first day at university, now feigning an ever-so-slightly German accent. The interactions make no sense. I go along with it at the time, but there is an exuberance and a lack of reasoning in his actions that is just a bit askew.

It's impossible to pinpoint when all the stuff with Dad began. It is one of the biggest kickers for families like ours when we try to remember. There's no beginning to mark, should we even want to pause, take stock and get our bearings.

But maybe this was it, decades before it got really bad. There. That moment in the car park. Early Nineties.

No, it had to be later. When he became obsessive about peeling onions before stacking them in the fridge in a neat wall to save space? Their brown gossamer skins troubled him as they were 'taking up too much room'.

But aren't dads just weird anyway?

That's their job. Being weird, embarrassing you and driving you places. And my dad loved to drive, although sometime in the Nineties he became mysteriously cagey about getting behind the wheel. Sometimes on the simplest trips, my mother said, he got completely lost.

The confused Finnish students disappear out of the car park.

Other Freshers wander past on their first day in Scotland carrying lava lamps and *Betty Blue* posters.

'They seem like a good bunch,' my dad says, not being American anymore. He was very proud that I'd got to uni. Even if he never quite knew what I studied. He was always proud of me – even years later, when he didn't 100 per cent know who I was.

'My only little girl, off to university,' he says, picking up a box.

Oh yes, his *only little girl* – he never stopped with that either.

'Do you think there is something wrong with Dad?' I said to Mam on the phone a few weeks after I left.

'What do you mean?' she said.

'Oh, just some of the stuff he does,' I said. 'It's like he's got dementia.'

'Oh, Grace, he's not got dementia,' she sighed. 'He's just a dickhead.'

* * *

This university campus that I'd made my new home felt oddly
adrift from the outside world. Built in the grounds of the
Airthrey Castle estate, our uni halls sat in the centre of 360
acres of greenery, overlooked by mountains and pelted by
rain almost twelve months a year. From September until
January the grassy knolls and forest glades behind our halls
of residence would fetch up a sumptuous scattering of potent
magic mushrooms. On news of a new crop ripening, students
would converge carrying old ice-cream boxes to commence
foraging. Soon, the sounds of Ozric Tentacles tormented the
corridors as we lay around on our beds with our ankles in the
air, beaming at the ceiling when we should have been finding
the magic realism in Woolf's *Orlando*. The first year passed in
a joyous blink until the grades arrived. Friends began going
home at weekends and instead of reappearing carrying their
wee nan's teeth-rotting tablet, they simply didn't reappear at
all, ever again, quietly throwing in the towel on uni life. Now
this frightened me. Going home was not an option. I had to
fix up, and sharpish.

1993

'The lead story should be that the tarmac is bought from
England. From Hull,' an irate student is telling us. 'It's not
even Scottish tarmac. We make tarmac in Scotland!'

At the second-year Welcome Meeting for the University of
Stirling student newspaper, I am having my first experience of

news. Inveigling my way into the world of print is very much part of my new five-year plan.

'The scoop is the waste of university money,' another agrees. 'We should put that on the cover. "Cash Squandered in English Tarmac Scandal."'

This is not going well. Journalism, if the last seventeen minutes are anything to go by, does not seem terribly exciting. It feels nothing like Piers Morgan's 'Bizarre' column where he'd have one arm around Bruce Springsteen by now and an exclusive on the Bros come-back. Instead, today's red-hot topics include: press ethics, whether the campus rabbit population should be subject to culling (they were eating all the campus chrysanthemums) and a heady debate over whether bunnygate is a better front page than the absolute scandal of the tarmac expenditure. Several of them are dressed as actual grown-ups in shirts, ties and pleasant sweaters.

'Is there any room for anything kind of, um, funny?' I ask, raising a hand.

'Such as?' says the editor

'Er, well, like satire, maybe.'

I don't really mean satire. I mean silliness.

I just know they'll go for satire because boring people since George I's reign have claimed to have a great respect for satire.

'Satire,' they all nod. 'Yes, satire.'

Bingo, I think.

'You could write something funny exposing this tarmac expenditure scandal for what it is? Like in "Rotten Boroughs" in *Private Eye.*'

'Um ...' I say, chancing my arm, 'I was thinking more like ... a column about campus life. About all the different tribes ... and, well, the gossip we're all talking about on a Sunday morning on our sofas.'

'We don't have a gossip column,' says a third year who has actual leather elbow patches on his jumper. 'Gossip is a bit naff.'

This may be true, but gossip is the lifeblood of the campus. We are 3,000 twenty-somethings living in a glorified nature reserve on the side of a mountain in sideways sleet. What else is there to talk about other than each other's business?

'Also,' says the editor, 'we can't go around printing things about people that aren't true.'

'Well, I wouldn't be making things up,' I say. 'Just printing what happened and taking the piss out of things a bit.'

I look hopefully at them as they stare back as if I've asked to whip off my top and bounce on a trampette on page three.

'Let's come back to that,' the third year says. Then a Fresher who smells of chlorine asks if he could write up the regional front-crawl heats happening at the uni pool and debate moves on to the recent verruca outbreak.

'Maybe that's the cover,' a voice says. '"Uni Wrongfooted by Verruca Scandal."'

I flounce out of the door, vowing never to darken their doors again. Not a soul notices.

* * *

At a loss, yet undeterred, next I hit up the drama club. Here things then went from bad to worse. The first meeting involved playing a long improvisation game of swapping hats and pretending to be at a bus stop – the memory of which still gives me atopic eczema. The goal that term seemed to be to stage *Waiting for Godot* by Samuel Beckett, despite my firm reasoning that audiences throughout time were only ever sitting through it out of politeness. Within a month, I had a strong sense that I was not cut out to hang with actor types. I just did not know where to look whenever someone in loon pants and leg warmers began hamming up Lady Macbeth's speech. From reading the newspapers I knew that the Cambridge Footlights seemed to propel folk like Emma Thompson and Stephen Fry from unknown students straight into the heart of the media establishment. But being with people like this gave me clues as to why there were so few working-class thespians. It was just so show-offy. I was fine with being pretentious in the privacy of my own head, but in public? With people looking? Writing felt much more like a job for me. That's showing off in private. But how?

Salvation beckoned weeks later: a piece of A4 paper stuck to a noticeboard in the English Department.

'Writers Wanted' for a new campus fanzine called *Mental Block*. This was a pun on the bleak, cell-like concrete-block rooms in which we all lived. I wrote down the number on my arm, took a deep breath and telephoned the editor. He was a boy called Keith, a gentle-sounding but mischievous third year. He wanted the fanzine to take an irreverent look at campus life. I liked the phrase 'irreverent look'. That, alongside 'sideways swipe' and 'backwards glance', was my favourite type of writing. He'd found a few other willing writers already. It sounded perfect. It sounded a tiny bit *Smash Hits*-y.

1994

During the spring term of 1994 I sat at my desk overlooking the western extremity of the Ochil Hills, typing nonsense into an electric typewriter. I wrote a 'cool or not cool' barometer – which was an idea blatantly thieved from *The Face* magazine – and also some silly lists (the word 'listicle' was yet to be invented). After printing out these particular slices of copy at the newsagent, I trimmed the words with scissors and Pritt-Sticked them back onto a blank A4 page, fitting them around blurry black-and-white pictures. The finished product was nothing short of horrible to look at. It was part *Smash Hits*, part kidnapper's ransom letter. It was festooned with spelling mistakes and blank gaps where the pieces didn't fit. I filled these holes with shit BIC-pen illustrations. My writing style was verbose and erratic and it leaned heavily on weak in-jokes that only seventeen people understood. The following decades didn't see me improve a great deal, but this was the rawest version. I delivered the pages to Keith by hand outside a pub and ran off before he could look at it. What if he didn't laugh?

'Do more,' said Keith the next day when I passed him in the corridor. 'It was great. There's more space to fill.' So I did.

My next contributions were bolder. I invented news items about the 'Balls Up' Juggling Club and the patient girlfriend clique who hung around the rugby boys. I wrote about the glamorous clique of Erasmus students and prolific shaggers. I wrote tips on how to feign blindness in a thin corridor towards someone you'd drunkenly fumbled at the Coors Beer Two-for-One night. I rated the private study booths on the top floor of the library in order of the most exhilarating to copulate in. None of this could I ever show my parents. Along the way, I began to develop a style – or, at least, I began to rob and recycle bits of the things I loved. There were elements of Karen Krizanovich's *Sky* magazine pithiness, plus the self-involved chuntering of Victoria Wood's Kitty from *As Seen on TV*. Victor Lewis-Smith, restaurant and TV columnist, was definitely in there too. I loved how Lewis-Smith, in print, played the part of a man just on the edge of his own sanity. Each time we erected a little trestle table in the main uni foyer to begin flogging copies of *Mental Block*, I fretted that no one would care, but then a crowd would appear and the issues began to vanish. Then, within the hour, a blowback of fury and giddiness and shrieking would begin about the things we had said. Yes, some people were piggin' livid, but most found it funny. And my name was printed all over it. The feeling was intoxicating. Better than any Class A. Better than a Brownie Badge or carrying a flag in church. Better, almost, than a letter printed in the *NME* defending Nicky Wire. When something you write strikes a chord and ends up widely read, it feels a bit, in your brain at least, like being loved. Particularly when you write silly things. Clearly silly things won't win you as many prizes as being serious; however, you only have to write *once* at a silly frequency that makes a stranger really snort with laughter and then you're in their hearts, just a little bit, forever. I'd take silly over serious any day.

Obviously over the next few issues, I began to push my luck. I wrote reviews of atrocious campus food and invented fake small ads for disgusting fake products. I took several pot shots at the Principal of the university himself, who was, according to my mushroom-addled pseudo-communist mind, both slothful and corrupt as well as a terrifying symbol of the petite-bourgeoisie establishment. It was quite a flight of imagination on my part, bearing in mind that the Principal was actually a terribly nice man called Alasdair whose main job was juggling teaching budgets. Thankfully, Generation X students were allowed to work organically through our stage of being nauseating little berks without it spoiling our futures. We could gob off, push people's buttons, flip-flop between beliefs and act atrociously without anyone screengrabbing the evidence and storing it in a folder as a weapon. We didn't know the Shangri-La in which we were living. After about a year, Keith, as the editor, was threatened with ejection from the campus without honours if we carried on. *Mental Block* ground completely to a halt for a while and then trickled on a little longer in a more prim, censored way, which upset nobody. This was no fun at all. All funny writing has to cause a little collateral damage. Then Keith graduated, taking his honours and running before the Principal could change his mind. Desperate to write something, I slunk back to the official student paper and begged them to let me write a less defamatory campus-life column called 'The Squealer'. Kindly, they gave me the time of day. Of course, by now, I yearned to spread my audience wider. *Cosmopolitan*, I read, were looking for 'student writers'. A competition in the back of one of the magazines offered a prize that included a trip to the Groucho Club to meet Marcelle D'Argy Smith, work experience at National Magazines in London and a chance to see your writing in their pages. They wanted a covering letter describing why I was the bright, vibrant young woman they needed and five feature ideas. One evening soon after, I drank half a bottle of Thunderbird, shoved a piece of A4 in my typewriter and bashed out the title 'Clitoris Allsorts: Ten ways to make your hotspot work for you *and him*.' It was a heinous title, but something told me it might get a reaction.

Easter Sunday, 1995

''Ere, have an Easter chicken tikka balti pasty,' Mam says, rustling inside a large brown paper bag. 'That'll cheer you up.' Easter in our house is like a directionless Christmas: the house fit to bursting with Whoops! gun-stickered hot cross buns and Mini Egg cookies, but no real schedule for eating them. Just freeform grazing.

The pasties, £1.99 for six, are from 'Market Street', an aisle at the back of Morrisons supermarket where the signage goes all mock Dickensian, as if you've taken a wrong turn by the tinned peas, stumbled through the mists of time and wound up in a magical Olde Worlde of baked goods. I pick up the pasty, aware without much thought that it contains approximately 320 calories. I cut the pasty in half, leaving the remainder inside the paper bag for someone else in the family to eat. In approximately one hour's time I will pass by in search of a pen and hoover it up to help with my sadness. *Cosmopolitan* do not care about my revolutionary thoughts on the clitoris. Two months have passed. No reply. I vow to myself I'll enter again next year and be grateful I still have my role at the student paper writing pithy words on the poor quality of scampi in a basket in the main bar. My self-confidence has reduced but the same cannot be said for my bottom.

'I'm putting weight on *again*,' I sigh to Mam. 'I'd just got a stone off after Christmas.'

'Oh, you're *volumptuous*,' Mam says, sounding out the errant 'm' clearly. 'Men like something to keep the bed warm.'

In my twenties I began in earnest my lifelong war against weight gain. The pounds slid on and I took them off again. Size sixteen in January, size ten by March, size twelve by April, back at twelve for June. Hungry, hungry, being good, eating again, fatter, hungry. When I am size ten, there is a size sixteen woman inside me dying to get out. She's in there. Cramped and hot and giddy with starvation, giggling at my conceit. 'I'll be back,' she laughs. 'Enjoy your defined décolletage and your neat waist ... I'll be fucking back.'

Binge-eating was not my style. Or filling my plate right up. Or over-ordering. Or eating late at night. Or ordering cartwheel-sized pizza deliveries and eating leftovers for breakfast. Or any of the ways thinner people think fatter people get fatter. In my twenties I ate smallish portions and was skilled at going without. But as my body filled out into curves, I already knew that if I wanted those magical Miss World measurements of 36-24-36, I would have a serious fight on my hands in this delicious, ever-changing new world of mega-processed food. You do not, I had begun to see, have to eat almost any of this stuff to put on weight. One thousand calories could pass in a few heavenly bites. Processed food is an extremely user-friendly, mega-efficient transference of fats and carbs down one's gullet. It's specifically designed this way. Extremely clever people in corporate test kitchens are paid top dollar to design each item to inspire joy and pleasure. These everyday heroes were wrapping chicken tikka balti pieces in shortcrust pastry and selling them at six for just short of two quid. Which mortal being could turn their nose up at this?

In Carlisle there were now two large ASDAs plus an enormous Tesco and a branch of Morrisons too. If grocery shopping in the Eighties had grown to be exciting, the Nineties sent it skywards. You could eat around the world. Continental and American deliciousness began to fill the aisles. I grew partial to Pom-Bears, Choco Leibniz and even glasses of

Sunny D. In advert breaks on Border TV aspirational types with Filofaxes skipped through airports. They lunched on San Marco frozen pizzas and smeared Boursin on baguettes at lunch. They hung out in Brooklyn diners eating frozen griddle waffles, stuffed-crust pizzas or bulging hotdogs with sweet yellow mustards. And it was all available here in the North *right now*. Yet, not only was this food foreign and exciting, it was also time-saving. You pulled it out of the freezer, shoved it in the oven or banged it in the microwave. It was quick. This was important, the adverts reminded us, as we were busy, busy people. Family life was often portrayed as stressed mothers and slightly dim dads in need of octopus limbs to cope with their demanding brood. These families needed Birds Eye Pan Flair and McCain 'Quickety Quick' Micro Chips. The Dents were particularly enchanted by a woman called Aunt Bessie – a benevolent freezer goddess who sweated over roast potatoes and Yorkshire puddings so we didn't need to. No peeling. No measuring. No whisking. Soon everything in Mam's fridge was so handy that we rarely cooked from scratch at all. I mean, imagine taking a peeler, scraping a carrot, chopping it and then cooking it in boiling water on a hob. I mean, what were we, Vikings? Why make a lasagne yourself when you can buy it for 99p in a plastic tray?

Perhaps the most convenient thing about microwave meals for many families was that they allowed us to grab our dinners separately. This allowed us all to avoid each other. For long spaces of time in Currock, our posh dinner table with the extendable leaves was mainly just a place to shove knick-knacks, petrol receipts and the ironing pile. Things that needed to be discussed together as a family could now be avoided for months or years. Some things that needed to be said were never tackled at all. My dad, who had started to slide on the pounds at this point, came in from work as late as he could, then ate microwaved liver and bacon on a tray facing rolling news on Sky.

'How was work, Dad?' I'd ask.

'Busy,' he'd say, with no further details.

Did Dad speak to his other kids anymore? None of us knew.

'Bring us the pepper, precious,' he'd say.

Now nearing his sixties, he was facing retirement. Lord knows how he would handle having nowhere to hide.

Britain may have now had food for busy people, but relatively speaking the pace of life was still rather gentle, no matter what the adverts said. Particularly in Carlisle, where Easter breaks passed so slowly I could hear my leg-hair growing. By Easter 1995, I was in the third year of a four-year Scottish degree and making a start on my final dissertation. Unless I made a plan soon for what to do after uni, I would need to go home. My *Cosmo* dreams were clearly over, and I'd just crashed and burned out of the second round of a search for trainee producers on zany, madcap Channel 4 morning show *The Big Breakfast* with Paula Yates, Gaby Roslin and Chris Evans. The twelve-page application form had rinsed me of every single brainfart I'd had about the show over the past three years. It cost me a seventy-quid return ticket to London, which was three whole Saturdays of my student job flogging Estée Lauder lipstick in Debenhams.

'Which uni?' a scrunch-faced woman called Fenella asked.

Her bare feet were up on the desk, with her dirty soles facing towards me. This felt a bit rude, but I reasoned it must be a London thing, and as she was the gatekeeper to my future happiness, I should greet it cheerily.

'Stirling,' I said, my plump, Kookai-wrapped left arse cheek perched on the corner of a chaise longue.

'Where's that?' she said.

'Scotland,' I said.

'Really?' she said. It felt like a bad start.

Fenella began the interview in haste.

'If we wanted to launch a hot-air balloon from the *Big Breakfast* garden tomorrow, who would you call?' she asked suddenly.

'Um, I would get *Yellow Pages* and find someone with a balloon and speak to them first,' I said.

'And?' she said.

'And ...' I said. 'Measure the *Big Breakfast* garden to give them details of space.'

'And?' she said, annoyed.

'Um ... I'm not ... I don't really ...' I said, having now exhausted everything I knew about balloons.

'Is that it?' she said, recrossing her feet and flexing her grubby big toes.

'Well, yes,' I said.

'Air traffic control!' she said manically. 'Would you not telephone air traffic control? They are the first people I'd call! You'd find the coordinates of the garden and alert air traffic control.'

'Would I not call the balloon expert first?' I mumbled.

'NO,' she said, and soon I was back at Euston Station, which was galling, as I'd planned to be wearing a vintage puff-ball dress and flirting with Rick from Shed Seven by 5 p.m.

On the train back to Carlisle in time for Easter Sunday, I felt foolish to have even tried.

'Oh, bugger them,' Mam said when I got back. 'Have this Mini Egg cookie. There's only one left in the bag. Look, it's lonely. Go on, you look hungry, eat!'

If I was going to be a media person, I needed to be brighter and cooler and cleverer – and I definitely needed a smaller bottom.

1996

Checking my newly re-bony décolletage in the mirror of my uni room, above the desk where my final dissertation sits awaiting its closing chapter, I remind myself that at least I am skinny again. No plan is in place for the future, but skinny takes the edge off everything. I wonder if my daily calorie allowance permits a Knorr Quick Soup. The one without croutons as the croutons are quite fatty. I'll have it with

Ryvita and low-fat cottage cheese, then head off to 'Float, Don't Bloat' aqua aerobics.

Earlier, on my way in to the posher, more grown-up halls of residence that students move into to write their final dissertations, I found a Post-it note attached to my door.

'*Your mother called. She says she will keep trying.*'

This does not seem good. It feels instinctively bad. The last time she did this was because Gran had passed away.

Now the shared payphone in the hallway is ringing again.

Mam sounds frazzled. She is on a payphone in the disembarkation hall in Southampton docks.

'Dad keeps getting dizzy,' she says. 'He was going into the cabaret bar on the ship the other night and his head went all waffy.'

'Was he tipsy?' I say.

Booze measures on these P&O Euro-cruises they keep going on are famously generous.

'No. Not really,' she says. 'I mean, we'd had some Irish coffees and a carafe of Merlot. And he'd had a couple of little beers, but he wasn't drunk.'

Mam and Dad, throughout their whole lives, never had proper hobbies. Or any sort of frivolous pastime. They worked and they watched a bit of telly and they slept. Holidays were mainly spent in England or at a push in North Wales. We went to Spain once in the Eighties by coach. It took days to get there, but our adventure was the talk of Currock. Sometimes my parents holidayed within twenty miles of Carlisle itself in a static caravan in Silloth-on-Solway overlooking the West Cumbrian coast. After retirement, with me and Dave gone, a new focus entered their lives: cruising.

''Ere, keep an eye out for Page 22 coming back round.' Mam has got the Teletext cruise pages on. She chucks me the remote control. 'It's just gone past, but it'll be back. Press pause if you see it!'

Mam's special skill was seeking out last-minute cruise bargains.

'Mam, there's 198 pages,' I'd groan, as the screen beeps and flashes with neon print.

'I know, but they come round fast, the little buggers,' she'd say. 'It's fourteen nights going out of Palma, for 256 quid, all-inclusive with a balcony! It's a good one!'

Although the thought of being stuck on a glorified ferry left me cold, my folks loved everything about this new nautical lifestyle. They loved the planning and the packing. It gave them something neutral to chat about. They loved the whole microclimate of being on ship with a thousand other like-minded sixty-somethings, taking Latin American ballroom dancing lessons and enjoying visits from celebrity chefs like James Martin or Gary Rhodes. The ship plodding methodically from port to port, with a schedule posted under their cabin door each night, appealed to my ex-army dad. You could see the Sphinx or the Leaning Tower of Pisa or Vatican City for two or three hours and, most importantly, be back in time for tea. Because the main thing they loved about cruising was the food. Delicious, plentiful food served 24/7: buffet breakfasts, elevenses, long lunches, afternoon teas by the pool, formal dinners and midnight top-deck pizza buffets. Getting your money's worth was easy. No passenger on a cruise went hungry.

Weight gain was a badge of honour. You could pile on ten extra pounds in a week. Dad packed different-sized trousers, some with elasticated waistbands, for the inevitable spread.

Dad's health had started to worry us all, in lots of little ways.

Since he'd retired he had grown plumper and certainly sleepier. Sometimes he even seemed a little confused. He'd given up driving. He wouldn't tell us exactly why. But I knew he'd had some sort of scare. Lately he was experiencing weird tingling sensations in his feet, as well as a constant thirst.

'This 'ouse is like a bloody sauna!' he'd roar. 'And she's always whackin' that immersion right up, making me parched.'

In the Seventies my dad was wiry in his army uniform. Now he had a definite belly. Pictures showed it protruding under the cummerbund he wore to shake hands with the Captain on formal dining evenings.

If you tackled Dad on his health, he became grumpy. So what if he slept in his chair all day and half of the evening?

'I've worked all my life,' he'd snap, eating a family-size bar of Fruit & Nut and slices of custard tart. 'Can you not just bloody let me be?'

This quickfire grumpiness worked well for him his entire life. He set the boundaries of what could be discussed. You'd try once or twice but then finally give up.

'So what happened then?' I say to Mam.

'The blue suitcase on the conveyer belt, George,' shouts Mam, with one hand muffling the phone. 'No, George! The blue one with the yellow ribbon on. That's ours. I've told you five times ... Well, we got him a seat and he righted himself eventually, but it was scary.'

'Can you go back to the doctor?' I say.

'Yes, we're gonna have to,' she agrees.

I should have stepped in here. Put a stop to the snacks. I should have nagged him to take up jogging too. Or at least walking. Dad's health was never quite right from around the mid-Nineties onwards. There was always something: his stomach, his joints, his balance. We needed to get him tested.

March 1996

'The problem would be with ulcers,' begins the posh man in the white coat. 'Raised glucose damages the nerves in the feet and this messes with the body's circulation.'

The specialist at the Cumberland Infirmary, just 1.8 miles across the city from ASDA, is lecturing us about too much sugar. He's drawn a rudimentary pair of legs on a piece of paper and is circling swirls and arrows around the shins. I try to listen and scribble things down, but there are a lot of long words and they're passing very quickly. If I get some down at least I could go to the uni library back in Scotland and look them up.

'This means,' he continues, 'that you can get cramps and weird pains in your toes and legs. Which is bothersome.' More doodling. We all lean forward to see.

'But the worst part,' he says, 'is that when the blood supply is poor it means cuts and sores do not heal. So these can turn to ulcers or gangrene.'

Dad nods. The specialist continues. We have seven and a half minutes of specialist appointment left and the waiting room is full.

'Obviously if that occurs this wouldn't be the end of the story,' the medic continues. 'We could try addressing some of the basic issues. We can remove all of the necrotic tissue, the peri-wound callus and foreign bodies right down to the viable tissue. That's simple enough, in theory. Then we can irrigate the wound with saline, dress it, blah-dee-blah. I mean, if it's an abscess, we'd need to drain it, whip away all the bad stuff ... and that's how we have the most success saving the limb. I have one patient, for example, who ...'

'I'm sorry, what?' I say.

The doctor carries on talking. My parents do not seem to notice the part where he's mentioned the possibility of chopping off my dad's leg.

'So the dilemma is making a choice and acting quickly,' the medic says. 'If we treat infection long-term with antibiotics, we merely increase the risk of amputation.'

'Hang on!' I jump in.

My parents bristle. They do not like it when I interrupt

doctors. Medical people are very important and we should simply nod gratefully when they talk.

'Amputation?' I say. 'We're not there now. He's just dizzy now. He doesn't have ulcers.'

'Oh,' says the doctor, 'yes. I was just explaining where poor diet and too much sugar leads. Sometimes. What we need to do in the meantime is lower Mr Dent's blood pressure, glucose and cholesterol. That's the key thing right now.'

'So no injections?' says Mam.

'No, not now,' the doctor says. 'Two pills a day. But please keep a close eye on blood sugar. If we crack that, this can be relatively plain sailing. But … it's curbing the sugar that patients do seem to have problems with.'

'Thank you, doctor,' says my dad, standing up, committing to nothing. I follow him out, deflated.

The specialist bids us goodbye, back out into the corridor. It's like he's done this spiel three times already today and will do it fifteen more before home time.

The mystery of Dad's dizziness, sleepiness and thirst is explained. At the age of sixty, within a decade of the big ASDA opening and a few years cruising the high seas – which I'm sure is entirely coincidental – Dad has developed Type 2 diabetes.

We mooch back to the car in silence.

'There's gonna have to be some changes,' Mam says, her voice trailing off as she's already fresh out of ideas.

'Dad,' I say seriously, 'you're gonna have to stop eating chocolate trifle every night. This is serious.'

Dad looks away as if I'm addressing someone else.

'I think the main problem I've got,' he says solemnly, 'is which poor bastard is gonna buy half of me socks?'

'Dad, it's not funny,' I say, even if it was very funny. This is one of the ways he distracts you.

'Oh, come on, precious,' he says. 'I'm gonna save a fortune on slippers.'

On the way home, I thought hard about the future. Going to London and pushing to be part of the media scene seemed like a waste of effort. That woman's bare feet up on the desk? The way she had no idea where my uni was? It spoke volumes. But if I were to come home for good after graduation, I could step in and care for Dad as he got old. That's what good daughters do. Especially ones from Currock, I thought. Girls like me can have ridiculous dreams, but at the end of the day, they should do the right thing.

May 1996

At a computer in the far corner of a science lab two of my nerdiest uni friends, Alan and Dirk, are in fits of filthy laughter, typing long chains of mysterious code into a keyboard. I'm supposed to be in the university twenty-four-hour study room finishing my dissertation – a 25,000-word post-modern discussion on Virginia Woolf and Rose Tremain. It felt like a good idea when I proposed it. Now, I'd rather watch moss dry on a radiator than write the conclusion.

Besides, I'm curious as to what's going on in this lab.

The monitor turns ominously black aside from some yellow spindly text. Then it requests another password. Then a page of a hundred or so lines of more code appears, underlined with neon. In years to come, I would know these as 'links'.

'Not the dog again,' moans Dirk.

'It's gotta be done,' says Alan, shaking his head.

'Dinnae show Grace the dog,' says Dirk.

'Show me the dog,' I say

I've seen the heady world of home computers on *Tomorrow's World* with Judith Hann. This is going to be some space-age computer-generated animation of a dog for me to smile at.

Alan clicks on some links and types a bit more. He claims to be connecting to another computer on the other side of the world. And then the screen fills with a set of photos, revealing themselves slowly.

A woman with long brown hair is having rather enthusiastic sex with a rather large Great Dane.

'What? No, noooooooo!' I cry, covering my eyes but then going in for a proper look. 'Who, what ... how did you get that?'

The boys – being horrible beastly boys – find this hilarious.

In that moment, I knew that something had changed. My friends really were, as they'd claimed several times, talking to strangers all over the world. They were swapping messages, pictures and files via computer using only the phoneline. Some of them were ridiculous top-grade smut, but mostly they were trading essays on Judas Priest and Led Zeppelin sheet music and talking about conspiracy theories with fellow nerds in West Coast America. The world seemed to be shrinking. Talking to America was now as simple and relatively cheap as talking to your friend down the street.

I've tried up until this point not to mention something very important about the Seventies, Eighties and most of the Nineties. It's been difficult, and I think I've pulled it off. However, one specific, absolutely crucial fact has been fizzing behind my eyes, which colours every single memory. Just like it does for all Generation X people telling a story about the past. We want to scream this fact continuously because it's the main reason why everything happened differently back then. We were living on a different planet.

You see, until this point, there was no Internet.

There. I said it. I'll say it again.

Back then, there was no Internet.

There was no Internet.

Did I tell you there was no Internet?

No, come back! It's important. Humour me.

If Generation X kids seem like creaky relics repeating the same news about our low-fi, offline youth, it might sound like we're saying it so younger people can count their blessings. But we're not. We're actually retelling ourselves, over and over again, because we can't quite believe it. We look at life now, and life back then, and we feel like time travellers.

We lived through an era when literally every single godforsaken moment of daily life, from opening our eyes, was just one million times more hassle; it was an administrative wilderness without search engines, GPS maps, group chats, YouTube, online dating, selfies, Amazon Prime and the other 175 things we didn't have that today alone have made things easier so far.

We remember long patches of nothingness between two issues of our favourite print magazine, with no more information available on pop culture. Or feelings of real, cut-off, no-contact separation when someone was out of sight. We remember rarely having a clue about the feelings of strangers, neighbours or celebrities. We remember people being mysterious, elusive, unavailable. And we remember not knowing things: how the definitive answer to the question we had in the shower that morning was probably on the top floor of a library in New York and we'd never know within our whole lifetime. We remember the large ringfences around important people and the intense sense of deference and hierarchy over who we could just approach and speak to. And how impossible it was to be seen or heard or noticed. This kept us all much more neatly in our lanes. We remember how it felt the very first time we were so bold as to send an electronic letter straight to the address of someone important – a journalist, a store manager, a popstar – and ... PING! One came back.

If we harp on and on and on about this time, it's because we feel like living history. We lived through the second Big Bang. It's like you're speaking to someone who was there when the wheel was invented, who until that moment spent two decades pulling everything around on an anvil.

As me, Alan and Dirk walked home from the laboratory, I realised why they were so smitten with computers. All the normal rules of getting stuff done seemed to fly out of the window. In the pigeonhole beside my door, there was a boring brown foolscap envelope addressed to me bearing a London postmark. It had taken ten days to reach Stirling. As a mode of communication, it already felt prehistoric. Inside, there was a letter with a bright-red masthead from National Magazines. I gasped, then grinned, then began to really panic.

July 1996

Up and down Wardour Street in Soho, in the West End of London, I walk in search of the capital's most celebrated showbiz private members' club.

'Is this the Groucho Club?' I shout to the glamorous receptionist, opening a large door with dark glass.

London door numbers always seem to have been given out during a gale. I'm already ten minutes late for the most important tête-à-tête of my life. We're having lunch, but I do not feel like eating. My toe is poking through my stocking foot, my stomach is churning, my ears are full of white noise. I'm in absolutely no state to meet Marcelle D'Argy Smith, the editor of *Cosmopolitan*.

After graduation, in June 1996, with 'Wannabe' by the Spice Girls blaring from every radio station and 'Girl Power' the hot topic of the summer, I moved back to my parents' place to sleep in the room where Mam kept her wallpaper table and spare cat litter. Despite my promises that I was just on the verge of finding employment, Mam encouraged me to try harder by intruding into the room at 7.05 a.m. each day to clatter the Venetian blinds and shout the names of nearby turnip-picking opportunities. She did not accept I was now an actual intellectual and would only consider employment that required a nuanced understanding of magic realism in Angela Carter's post-feminist fiction.

'You can be an intellectual at Southwaite!' she yelled, waving me off to clear tables at the Granada service station on the M6. This job involved eight-hour shifts of being shouted at by the public over the price of English breakfasts and being sexually harassed by the chef with finger tattoos, which I should have complained about but it actually broke up the day.

From Carlisle, I'd written a begging letter to a man called Toby Young who had started a high-brow, low-culture magazine called *Modern Review*. He politely rejected me as his assistant. I'd also tried for a BBC broadcast news intern position, which involved a group interview at the Jurys Pond hotel, Glasgow, which was a terrifying cross between *Press Gang* on CITV and *Lord of the Flies*. Now, as I turned up at the Groucho Club, I had one lifeline left. An invite to have lunch with Marcelle, Queen of Glam Fash Mags. In my final year, after my second attempt at the *Cosmo* competition, they'd called me up out of the blue and asked if, as a student, I fancied writing a very small 200-word segment on Prozac usage among female students. This was around the time of Elizabeth Wurtzel's first book, *Prozac Nation*; being female and a massive headcase had suddenly become quite trendy. I'd sent them a little piece and they'd allotted me a non-paid role with the lofty title 'student advisor'. I wasn't sure what this meant at all, but it sounded grand. Then an official letter arrived asking me to lunch with Marcelle herself. As I lay the night before on a blow-up mattress on my brother's floor in his squat in Hackney, I struggled to think how I'd fake it as a cool, connected media chick who just casually lunches on Dean Street with an editor. My outfit wouldn't cut it for a start; a Morgan De Toi skirt made of ruched fake taffeta fabric and a Jane Norman fitted top. I'd look like an interloper. And not, say, an executive producer from Channel 4 here to meet Ben Volpeliere-Pierrot for langoustines.

Photos of the Groucho's inner sanctum were never available, but I imagined it to be a dark, smokey set of uncarpeted rooms chock full of the British cognoscenti. Damon from Blur would probably be on the piano clanking through 'Park Life', with Muriel Grey, clad in a leather mini skirt, discussing the Young British Artists with Tom Paulin. Midway through my first martini, Damien Hirst would waltz in to rapturous cheers, stinking of formaldehyde, then as one we'd unite for a rousing chorus of 'First We Take Manhattan' by Leonard Cohen. It would be totally bohemian and I'd fit in just marvellously and learn to be bohemian too. Some years would pass before I accepted that my type of working-class people are really not suited to being bohemian, as bohemian really means chaotic, self-destructive, whimsical and a bit whiffy. Most North London bohemians would be a lot happier if they stopped wife-swapping and got a nice 'To Do' list on the go; then their homes might be full of neat rows of fabric-conditioned socks, rather than self-involved sobbing, cat piss and orchids.

A gang of men checking in at the same time as me are dressed in dogtooth suits and thick bottle glasses. They are all various versions of Chris Evans from *Don't Forget Your Toothbrush*. This gang disappear into a dark side door on the left on the ground floor where a loud lunchtime boozing session seems to be in full swing. Meanwhile, the receptionist points me skywards.

'*Cosmopolitan* lunch?' she says. 'Top-floor suite. Follow the other girls.'

What other girls?

As I walked nervously up the three flights of stairs, there was a small nagging truth at the pit of my stomach that I needed to put a sock in. I didn't really like *Cosmopolitan* magazine. In fact, all women's mags had begun to lose their shine by now. My childlike faith in their mantras about 'having it all' was on the wane. As a teen, these magazines gave us girls a sneaky glimpse at what it's like to be a real adult lady. It looked brilliant. By my mid-twenties I'd be wearing three shades of eyeshadow during the daytime, eating a lot of honeydew melon to replenish my water levels and dating men who fancied unconventionally pretty girls who made up for it with feistiness and brains. I'd have a lovely apartment with coordinated scatter cushions, my career would be on the rise and I'd spend weekends mini-breaking in European capitals or having second dates in country meadows, for which I'd chuck together a salad featuring three types of leaf: lollo rosso, rocket and watercress. Sexually, I'd be at it constantly, four times a week, in six positions that coordinated with my star sign. Despite being in the boardroom every other week asking for more money, I'd also know 'when the time was right' to have babies. They never mentioned women like me who loved being handed a cute baby but loved more the moment I could hand one back, swathed in relief that the feeling of anxiety and responsibility wasn't permanent. The more I read glossy magazines the less I felt like a woman. More like a curious bystander. I needed to really keep this quiet.

The best thing about the *Cosmo* lunch was how proud it made Mam.

'Our Grace is off to work for *Cosmo*,' she told the other mams in Morrisons, unless they spotted her first and went and hid behind the Eccles cakes.

'Marcelle D'Argy Smith, the editor of *Cosmopolitan*,' Mam would say, 'she asked for our Grace *in person*.'

I open the door. And there she is. She is not alone. This is by no means a tête-à-tête. There are fifteen other girls here.

At the far end of a large oval table, looking like a glorious high-sea captain, Marcelle D'Argy Smith stands wearing a navy blazer, a nude Breton-style jumper and navy culottes. She is as tiny as a fawn. A perfect mini-sized woman.

I had never seen her like, although I would grow accustomed to these forces of nature over the years: Tina Weaver, deputy editor of the *Mirror*, clip-clopping across the newsroom in her Giuseppe Zanotti heels. Ad guru Sly Bailey, imperious in Hervé Léger. There is extraordinary power in an expensively pulled together woman. A mensch with all her aesthetic plates spinning at once. Marcelle, for example, had that specific genre of hair that media women possess, which needs not one hairdresser but three different specialisms: one person who cuts, one person who colours, one who comes to your house to blow-dry at 7 a.m., after your tennis lesson but before your 10 a.m. cosmetic launch breakfast at The Ivy.

Her pink-ash manicure was offset by a chunky gold Rolex watch. Her jawline was razor sharp, with no under-flapping wobble, and her sharp cheekbones jutted upwards like two signposts to the gods. Marcelle was the type of perfect woman who, when I stand next to her, makes me feel like a diplodocus jumping into a child's sandpit, hoping to play nicely, but instead maiming the residents. Still, however intimidated I felt, and however I felt about women's magazines, I wanted to be in this sandpit.

Marcelle's long eyelashes flap as she humours the gaggle of hot young things in smart-casual clothes. As a Northern working-class woman, I will always be exceptionally bad at smart-casual. I just don't have the bone structure. I'm either 'smart' (a bit like Imelda Marcos) or 'casual' (going to the tip). I manage to take a seat at the far end of the table with no one noticing.

This is a group lunch of competition winners. How have I missed this?

At my end of the table, the girl beside me is chatting about sailing. Not sailing as in seven nights all-inclusive around the Med with your own porthole, but sailing *in her family's yacht*. The other girls chat confidently about steady boyfriends, intriguing fourth-round interviews, their shorthand skills and their places on post-graduate print journalism courses.

What? I need *another course* on top of my degree?

Most alarmingly, they all seem to have sorted out place-ments at the magazine.

Can you just do that?

Don't you have to wait to be asked?

Then lunch arrives and things get much worse.

'*Carré d'agneau,*' murmurs a waitress, placing an angular section of lamb, ribs protruding, the lower side leaking blood, in the space before me. It comes with a small silver terrine of white gloop, which she informs me is '*pommes aligot*'.

Pomme à la go?

Quickly cooked apples?

Why didn't I listen properly in French?

There are at least four choices of knives and fork.

What would Aunty Frieda do? I think.

I sneak a quick spoon of the white stuff into my mouth. It's cheesy mash.

This is all fine, I am supposed to be here, I tell myself quietly.

The lamb sits on the plate, glowering back at me. This is nothing like the lamb my mother makes, wrapped loosely in foil and whacked on a low heat for four hours. It looks like an autopsy with a garnish. It's bloody and sharp and green in places. I take the knife and fork and begin at the west wing of the beast, realising quickly that this fat and flesh are rock hard. I regroup and attack again between the boney ribs. Blood oozes across the plate. It is raw.

'Oh, I love it *rare*,' one of the girls says.

You can eat raw lamb? How do I not know that?

Back then there were a million things I didn't know about the world of fancy food. Thank God I didn't. If I'd known about the rules of etiquette and the faux pas waiting to trip me up, I'd never have left my bedroom.

After ten minutes of sawing and chewing and listening to a girl with a blonde bob tell us about being up in a helicopter with CNN, I've eaten two forkfuls of hard lamb fat with a powdery herb crust. Either my plate is getting fuller or I am getting smaller. Smaller and smaller with every bite, like Mrs Pepperpot.

'I really feel like I'm in the presence of some very special young women.' Marcelle gestures to a girl wearing a Chanel jacket over a floaty vintage Ghost dress who is off on a trip to Malawi to build an AIDS hospice with her bare hands before returning to her internship at the magazine.

'You were lucky,' one of Marcelle's assistants says to her. 'You got the last free space. We're booked up until next year.'

A large piece of wispy sage has wrapped itself around my back tooth. I try to dislodge it with my tongue, while nodding and smiling. As Marcelle leaves, after the main (which she didn't eat) and before pudding, I know that not only have I not spoken to her, as I was too shy and completely intimidated, but I will never see her again.

In the BHS café in Oxford Street, down the road from the Groucho, I ordered an all-day breakfast and somewhere between the beans and the fried bread I had a little cry. I knew a good daughter would stay close to her dad as his health declined, but I also knew that, despite the disaster of that *Cosmo* lunch, the lure of London and the media life was huge. I thought about the catch-22 of paying rent every month without work, but not being able to work without any experience of actually working. Then I thought about Marcelle D'Argy Smith striding into the Groucho Club with her just-stepped-out-of-a-salon hair, all heads turning as she moved around the room, brimming with power and steely charisma.

As I lifted the delicious life-restoring beige stodge to my mouth, the answer seemed clear. I had to jump one way or the other, and I chose London. No matter if I had nothing to come here for. Or anywhere to stay aside from Bob's floor for a few nights (I couldn't impose on him for longer than that, no matter how kind he was about it). I needed to pack a bag and come to London for good. But I was going to have to toughen up. And stop being so polite. And start lying. Really, really lying.

CHAPTER 5

By Royal Appointment

October 1996

'So you've worked for *Cosmopolitan*?' says the deputy acting features editor, looking at my CV.

'Yes,' I lie.

I'd never set foot in the *Cosmo* office and a woman called Camilla wasn't returning my phone calls about placements. I knew that a real go-getter would pitch up at Nat Mags reception and beg, but I was far too proud. I'd decided to change tactics and send letters begging for work to every magazine in the address section of the Amateur Writers' Yearbook.

'Are you one of the London City print journalism post-grads?' the woman asks. She's chucked my CV on the pile by now so doesn't seem likely to check. Her desk was a chaotic mess of press releases, empty Cup-a-Soup sachets, receipts and dying pot plants. She looked like she needed help.

'Um, yes,' I mumble.

'And you live in London?' she asks.

'Yes, I do,' I say more confidently.

I had seventy-five quid in my purse, a one-way ticket to Euston, an almost maxed-out credit card and a shabby suit-case full of 'nice work blouses' from Next. I was currently living on the outskirts of North-west London on borrowed time, cat-sitting for a friend of a friend in Mill Hill. The tenant hadn't warned me that all four cats brought live frogs through the cat flap with great enthusiasm and that it would be commonplace to wake with a live frog in bed with me or decapitated on my pillow. These animals were the polar opposite of emotional-support pets. I sent emails on a cranky library computer to editors during the day and read a free newspaper called *Loot* every night, circling ads for flats that either did not exist or were veiled invitations to enter the world of sex work, which I was beginning to feel was really all a 2.1 BA Hons in English equipped me for. I could dissect passages of Beowulf while waiting for trade.

'Can you do shorthand?' says the acting deputy features editor.

'Mmm-mmm,' I mumble.

'Do yer'wanna Hobnob?' she asks.

'Yes, please,' I say.

This bit wasn't a lie – I'd lived mainly on Frazzles and cans of Diet Lilt for three weeks. I was starving.

From the hundreds of magazines I'd dispatched 'electronic letters' to begging for work, *Chat* magazine was the last one I'd expected to hear from. Or had ever considered working for. If *Cosmo* was considered the strutting peacock at the top of the magazine parade, *Chat* was generally considered to be

down in the gutter with the earwigs. While *Cosmo* had Cindy
Crawford on the cover and features on matching your career
to your erogenous zone, *Chat* had an everyday-looking lass
with her gob open as if she, too, was amazed at the cacophony of working-class misfortune emblazoned on the cover.
Home hair-dye kits that had burned eye sockets, hen-
weekend punch-ups, villainous stepdads and women who'd
climbed onto the roof to waggle their Sky dish during
EastEnders and blew away into next door's paddling pool.

But I understood the lives of *Chat* ladies much better than
those of *Cosmo* women. *Chat*-world was where I grew up.
Every street in Currock was resident to an eccentric or a
family from hell. It was my mam's daily job to try and instil
in my mind some sort of class distinction between me and
Shanice Hastings ten doors down, with the dad who bred
Jack Russell puppies. We might not be as posh as Darlene
Phillips's lot with their SodaStream and breakfast bar, but
we were more hoity-toity than the Hastings family. They
didn't even have a vestibule. Their living room was right in
off the street.

'Don't let me catch you in Shanice Hastings' house!' she'd
scream. 'They're common as muck. I don't like how that dad
of hers always walks about with a bag of sheep's eyeballs.
Don't tell me they're for the dogs.'

'But, Maaaaaaam, Shanice's house is fun.'

Me and Shanice spent Easter weekend 1982 robbing Mace
Line Super Kings out of her nan's handbag and learning to
double-draw. Shanice would definitely buy *Chat* – she'd shove

it through your letter box afterwards with the word search done, so you didn't need to buy it too.

The acting deputy features editor looks me over, dressed up in my best weird office attire, with a tangle of split ends and chipped nail polish.

'If you did maternity cover for us for a few weeks, you'd be writing up the real-life stories,' she says. 'You interview readers, then write up their stories in house style but in their own words.'

I nod furiously.

'You know what that means?' she asks.

'Yeah,' I lie.

Lying gets easier the more times you do it. This is how Dad must feel all the time, I thought.

'The rough facts are on a form they've filled out,' she continues. 'But you need to call them and tease the details out of them. We need at least six stories per issue, fifty-two times per year, so it's busy. Are you good on the phone? Do you like to have a chat?'

I *loved* to have a chat. No lies there.

'Sorry, the stories come from where?' I ask.

'The form in each week's magazine. We pay £100 a story. Sometimes more. Today's mailbag is over there,' she says, nodding at two enormous mail sacks next to the filing cabinets.

Each week in the back of *Chat* magazine, and many other women's weekly mags, there was a headline that read 'Do you have a story? We pay £100 cash for your real-life tale!' Then some questions, such as, 'Say in your own words what happened ...' and 'Are you happy to be photographed?' The lure of this £100 was strong. *Chat* magazine was, it seemed, topping up electricity meters and buying bags of Iceland fishcakes in housing estates the length and breadth of Britain.

'Look,' she says, 'if you're not too busy with all your *Cosmopolitan* work, could you do the next two weeks? That's ten shifts. We pay fifty quid a day.'

And in that moment, I officially entered the glamorous world of the media.

On my first day at King's Reach Tower, I grabbed the silver mail bag and pulled it towards the desk and turned it over. At least 300 envelopes fell onto the floor. As I opened them and began to read, I started to file them into the regular themes: 'Tattoo gone wrong', 'Wedding brawl', 'Boyfriend tried to kill them' – that last pile was quite big, almost as big as the one I called 'Double life'. Britain seemed full of men with a similar approach to facing the truth as my dad. Funeral wakes across the land, it seemed, were regularly ruined by mistresses kicking off by the potted meat baps. Coffins were prised open last minute to grab back jewellery. Conmen, fantasists and bigamists were rife. This put my father's behaviour into perspective. I mean, he'd only lied for almost all of my life about two secret children. Actually, three secret children.

That wasn't so bad, was it?

Or maybe every day, in different ways, I got better at making excuses for him.

In the few years since I'd learned about my sisters and other brother, I'd wondered a lot about the ones who were left behind. I worried about how their lives had worked out. But I also felt oddly disloyal to Dad for worrying about them or wanting to forge a relationship. I loved the idea of having sisters. But Dad liked things as they were: all on his terms, no fuss, no blame, no comeback. Also, he was the ill one now. He was the one we should worry about.

'As the key turned in the lock, I knew it must be Sheila back with the prawn crackers and the vino,' I typed.

After my first fortnight at *Chat* I was getting rather good at this real-life business. I was invited back to cover more holidays and maternity leaves.

'We always had a girlie night in on Thursdays to discuss fellas. But when I smelled diesel oil I knew something was wrong. It was our Kevin back early from jail ...'

'*Jesus Christ*,' coughed Karen, the other staff writer, ricocheting back in her chair. 'Not again.'

'What's up?' I said.

'We did a health spread last year on STDs,' she said. 'Ladies keep sending in, um, samples for us to examine, wanting our opinion. It's another pair of pants.'

She picked up a pencil and fished a pair of used women's knickers out of the envelope and put them directly in the bin.

This was not the glitzy life I'd promised myself when I came to London to be a national treasure. Still, at the end of the first week, they'd put £350 into my bank account. One of my colleagues warned me that I'd have to pay something weird called pay-as-you-earn tax out of this in the future, which made no sense at all, but who cared about that? Right then I was the richest I'd ever been.

Rich and totally starving.

June 1997

The Friday-night kicking-out-time queue for the beigel shop on Brick Lane, East London, spills out of the glass door and into the street. I'm with my friend Clare, propped against the sticky shelf that runs along the wall inside, eating an onion platzel with chopped herring.

This type of thing was new to me. There were very few Jewish people in Cumbria in the Seventies. Or the Eighties or the Nineties. Or for that matter many Caribbeans or Indians or Bengali folk or Greeks or Turks or … well, anyone who wasn't more or less like me. And although I cannot sum up neatly why Carlisle stayed so pale and Protestant, the plain truth was, people of colour and different faiths rarely found themselves in Southwaite Services car park, ten miles from the Scottish border, pelted by sleet from Shap Fell saying brightly to each other, 'Fellas, *this* is the place.'

The demise of the factories throughout the Eighties didn't help. Or the fact that if you did set up home, being the very first family representing your skin tone or culture would inevitably be exhausting. All these things and others meant that, aside from the Renuccis, some Italians who owned chip shops in the area, and the well-loved Chung clan, who gave Cumbria its very first chow mein, I came from a landscape peopled almost exclusively by Anglo-Saxons within a few miles of Hadrian's Wall. And I'm not saying white people's food wasn't delicious – my fat little thighs throughout the Eighties, swelled by rock buns and Tizer, were proof that it was – but when I moved to London I realised I'd been missing out on a lot. Like beigels and chollah and platzels.

Clare and I are slightly inebriated and discussing a guy called Larry I've just met in Happiness Stan's on the Farringdon Road – a club made up of four rooms, playing 'an eclectic mix', as London folk say. My friends down south all love the drum-and-bass room; I think it sounds like being chased by bees. Regardless, David Bowie has been seen at Happiness Stan's, and although we missed him, we definitely saw Robbie Williams. Clare is my first proper London friend. She's a Manc who arrived in the South before me and is currently freelancing at *Mizz* magazine. She is slender and tall, with a shock of brown curly hair right down her back, and wears tailored wide-legged trousers. We drink gin and tonics in the Stanford Arms next to the IPC Magazines tower, flirt with the boys from *Loaded*, buy Melon Berry Snapple cocktails and Otis Spunkmeyer cookies for breakfast and plan our route to the top of the media tree. Clare once did work experience at *The Face*, which is quite possibly the coolest thing I have ever heard. Although even more magically, she knows about this wonderful thing called 'the guest list', where with just a little prior wrangling you can breeze into parties and nightclubs for free. You can sip fizzy plonk from trays near the door, make the correct noises at the public relations person who is footing the bill, rub elbows with a famous person off the telly like Mark Lamarr or Sanjay off *EastEnders* and then scoot off again without paying a penny to anyone. Gratis. Free. Complimentary bars are commonplace in London media land. It blows my mind. Especially as everyone behaves so relatively well, taking a couple of glasses, then leaving. If they set up a free bar somewhere in Carlisle every weekday evening at least one person would stay until they had wet themselves. I am working on moderating my alcohol intake.

'Larry worksh in the patissherie section at Harrodshh,' I slur, wiping chopped herring off my face, having drunk at least five glasses of cheap white wine at a private gallery viewing. This was before we'd even reached Alphabet Bar on Beak Street and ordered some très à la mode glasses of vodka and cranberry juice.

'Does Harrods even have a patisserie section?' she asks.

'It's in the food hall,' I say airily. 'He's a trained pastry chef.'

I knew this as I'd been to the food hall during one of my first weekends in London, just so I could walk in, like Aunt Frieda, with my shoulders back, feigning that I thought eleven quid for a loaf of bread made with 'ancient' grains was normal.

As Clare sips tea from a polystyrene carton, I begin shoving a piece of apple strudel into my head. The no-nonsense woman behind the counter is slicing a mountain of gelatinous salt beef. In the backroom kitchen, men hurl bags of flour into a giant mixer, chucking in jugs of water, yeast and salt. Soon circular lumps of beigel dough appear, plunge into boiling water, then rest on wooden boards before being shoved in the oven. Sammy Cohen's shop, at this time of the morning, is full of happy drunks and sad drunks. It's jampacked with smooching couples, hungry taxi drivers, the Met police night shift and a steady stream of miscellaneous night-time weirdos. I love this about London: things stay open. Sometimes all night long. As Dad always says about Carlisle, 'It's a nice place, princess, but you need to be home by seven cos that's when they take the pavements in for the night.'

'When is Larry ringing?' says Clare.

'Tuesday,' I say, flexing my new chic Nokia Aida 8146, rented from the One2One in Wood Green Shopping City.

A man waiting four entire days before contacting you – by telephoning to speak in person – is completely normal. Sure, my new phone has an option called SMS, which sends and receives text messages, but only an absolute weirdo would send one of those. And this gap between meeting Larry and hearing from Larry will transpire, when I look back on it, to be one of the best parts of the dating game. Human beings didn't appreciate its pureness at the time. We thought the wait was agony, which it was, but the time between meeting someone in a club and setting eyes on each other was often deliciously long and filled with knowing barely an iota about each other. No texts, no Facebook, no LinkedIn, not even Myspace. You were in an information drought with only your imagination to fill in the gaps. By Sunday night I won't even be sure what Larry looks like anymore. Meeting up will essentially be a blind date. Nevertheless, this is how people met the loves of their lives.

For what it's worth, Larry the artisan baker did not turn out to be the love of my life, but he was incredibly good fun on the three dates we went on – until I pushed him to bring me some of those super-expensive Harrods patisserie treats he was making By Royal Appointment for Her Majesty. Then he became vague. After three weeks of wild passion, Larry went quiet, so, imagining he'd not paid his mobile phone bill, I called the landline number he'd given me for emergencies.

'He's down Tesco's,' his flatmate said.

'OK, tell him I'll call when he gets back from shopping,' I said.

And his mate said, 'No, he's not shopping. Larry works in Tesco.'

'Pardon?' I said.

'Oh God,' the flatmate said.

So I pushed him a bit further and it turned out Larry was not an artisan baker; he was a shelf-stacker in the big Tesco on the Old Kent Road.

'He's going to kill me,' the flatmate said, his voice trailing off.

I never heard from Larry again. He did not return my calls. He was probably off making imaginary cakes By Royal Appointment to woo other women until he got busted. In absolute fairness, I had another lad in Clapham on the go anyway. And I wasn't an important contributing editor at *Cosmopolitan* magazine. We all got away with this kind of thing a lot more in the Nineties. The Internet ruined a lot.

October 1997

'How's it going, presh? I'll get Mam,' Dad says.

I can hear *A Touch of Frost* playing on the TV in the background. Calling home makes me homesick, although not enough to ever want to go home. I've not been back for a year.

'Are you OK, Dad?' I say. 'Are you sticking to your diet?'

'Oh yeah,' he says. 'Mam's got me on a regime. Are you looking after yourself? Are you being a good girl?'

'Yeah,' I say.

The best thing about me and Dad is that we let each other lie.

In the first twelve months of living in London, along with a small group of female cohorts – Eleanor, Clare, Billie, Lucy, Sophie – I have been anything other than the dictionary definition of good. The previous Friday night we'd been permitted to use the IPC advertising department's private box at the Albert Hall to see a Geordie kids' television duo called PJ & Duncan, aka Ant and Dec, who'd had some pop hits and were finishing their tour with a triumphant sell-out London gig. After draining dry the endless free champagne that comes gratis with a posh Albert Hall corporate box and dancing to 'Let's Get Ready to Rhumble', me and my gang of girls infiltrated a small, private friends 'n' family after party. In a drunken haze, I was caught helping myself to Dec's mam's favourite wine and speedily identified as neither Ant's nor Dec's cousin and chucked out onto the street by two security guards. Undeterred, I dusted myself off, gathered my troops and cabbed across to the Leopard Lounge in Fulham, where we convinced John Leslie from *Blue Peter* to throw us a party at his palatial Barnes mansion. Oddly, he complied, and soon we were all in his lounge as he DJ'd for us by playing his CD single of 'Professional Widow' by Tori Amos again and again, while I necked shots of tequila and slid down the stairs on the back of a framed poster of Cannon & Ball in panto. I left at 7 a.m., stopping the minicab driver halfway down the drive so I could be sick in John Leslie's hedge. I did not mention this to Dad. Neither did I tell him about the Friday before when I'd ended up at a *Loaded* magazine party and made friends with glamour models Jo Guest and Linsey Dawn McKenzie. Or the other Fridays I wound up at Browns nightclub in the West End with my friend, a model called Michelle, chancing my arm at its varying levels of VIP room, each one smaller and more difficult to get into than the last until I reached the top layer, which was just a broom cupboard with Martine McCutcheon and Sophie Atherton drinking bottles of Sol with Mick Hucknall. None of these things did I tell my dad about. And I was especially secretive about the fact that my credit card bill was now somewhere over £6,000. Each time I paid off a lump of the debt via a set of freelance shifts, the credit card company kindly wrote to extend my credit. First to seven grand, then to eight. Wasn't that nice of them? And ever so handy, as I did not want to ever go home. Life in London felt like starring in *Smash Hits*, not reading it.

And there was another important reason why I was never going back: after a year of being in the big city, I knew for sure that until then I'd been missing out on a lot of great food. After twenty years short of heat and colour and joy, I was now living in one of the most delicious cities on earth. Yes, I very often had an empty purse and a nose full of black bogies, but I was also living somewhere where food allowed me to feel the extremities of taste and texture. How could I go back to Carlisle now I'd fallen in love with the slimy pink lox and pungent mashed herring at Sammy Cohen's all-night beigel shop? Or Korean gochujang sauce over a bowl of bibimbap? Or fierce Scotch Bonnet chilli, hiding in a plate of ackee and saltfish? I loved chow mein, but I also *now* loved pho, ramen, udon and fideu. I loved spending Sunday afternoons in Chinatown, down Gerrard Street, consuming bowls of dark, wobbly, cloud ear fungus in vinegar, savouring the spongey bittersweet mushroom as it slid down my gullet. I'd begun to see that eating out was every bit as much fun as pubbing or clubbing or partying. It was maybe more fun. I'd started reading the pithy restaurant critic Michael Winner in the *Sunday Times* each weekend. His life sounded amazing. Winner loved dinner so much he'd made an entire life from it, and that was the name of his column. 'Winner's Dinners' was so well known that angry chefs even put signs in restaurant windows in Covent Garden that read: 'This is a Michael Winner-free zone.' The more he snarked, the more readers like me loved him.

How the hell, I began to wonder, did you become a restaurant critic? In fact, how did you get any of the good jobs in writing? There seemed to be a secret way in which these amazing roles were being handed out.

'So you're looking after yourself, precious?' asks Dad.

'Yeah, I'm doing good,' I said.

It wasn't the full story, but neither of us ever told each other that.

October 1998

At around 1.15 p.m. each day in the highly unglamorous IPC Magazines staff canteen, four or perhaps five fantastic, confident and deliciously self-important women would appear, and I'd watch them from behind my plate of chips. I was doing shifts covering staff-writing at a women's weekly called *Eva* – a sort of semi-ladette version of *Woman's Weekly*. I'd been writing a back-page, first-person column called 'Eva on the Couch', in which the fictitious Eva talks about her love life and friends. My byline was in a minuscule font and printed vertically, close to the staples on the side of the page. However, I didn't care, as this was probably the first time since university that I'd written anything that allowed me to be a bit funny. The sub-editors were even leaving in some of my funnier turns of phrase. It was like a lightbulb had switched on in my head.

Trying to be funny in women's magazines in the Nineties was hell. Jokes, by their very nature, require a writer to be specific in their use of words. Each cultural reference, turn of phrase or brand name in a punchline is chosen with care. Being funny is a science. A 'campervan' isn't funny, but 'a Vauxhall Rascal' is. The phrase 'I drank until I couldn't see straight' is not funny. 'I drank until I was doing press-ups outside the pub to impress some lads' is much better. When a woman wrote funny things for magazines in the Nineties, she would often see it trimmed and steamrollered back into 'house style'. I found it exasperating. Surely there were more women out there like me?

In the canteen, the gang of tall, glamorous women with small waists would cavort past my table wearing belted trench coats and tweed skirts. These women never seemed to wear make-up; they just had fresh, clean skin, cheekbones and blue eyes. Their tastefully blonde or mousy hair was tucked neatly behind their ears. Their canteen tactic was to commandeer a large table at the back, before approaching the hatch one by one to scan the metal terrines of catering-company-supplied mush. They did this, always, while frowning, as if each lunch-break was their first time ever seeing macaroni cheese, and each time they were newly appalled.

Eventually one would return with a plate of dressed chickpeas and a green salad. Then another would venture off and return with a small bowl of the soup of the day and an unbuttered roll. Or perhaps merely a big pile of green runner beans.

I asked the *Eva* girls who they were, but the names I was told couldn't possibly have been true. They sounded a bit like this: 'I think that's Taffeta Flinty-Wimslow and Araminta Losely-Glossop, and the one in the cape is Laurence Chevalier-Ducarte.'

They were the girls from *Marie Claire* magazine. And they were amazing. I stared at them like a child with her nose up at the sweetshop window. Although *Marie Claire* was part of the IPC Magazine family, they worked in their own separate building across the road from the high rise. These women were living the dream: they appeared on morning television shows giving their opinions on fashion, beauty, showbusiness or current affairs. I often spotted them getting out of black cabs with teams of assistants rushing to gather their suitcases. Sometimes you'd see them marching down Stanford Street to the office, frequently carrying a huge bunch of flowers or at least three impressive-looking goodie bags.

All this made me take stock of my life. Winter was coming and I was living in a shared flat in Bounds Green at the end of the Piccadilly Line above a building merchant's, with dodgy floorboards in the hallway that I had on one occasion fallen through with both feet up to the waist. I was scurrying off to the Piccadilly Line before sunrise most mornings and standing up in rush hour, dangling off a handrail in a fetid broth of builders' morning farts and hangover breath, and doing the same thing in reverse many evenings, but now with hair that emitted filthy grey grease puddles in the shower. I was dating a guy called Nik – with a k – who was starting his own Internet dot-com firm in Shoreditch and was nice enough but clearly still in love with his ex and also had a latex fetish, which I did not. This did not stop him turning up for dinner at Andrew Edmunds with rubber underpants on under his Moschino trousers, shouting, 'I have the pants on now!'

It put me right off my risotto.

I was also writing for a small free magazine called *Girl About Town*, which let me do a small profile of a new comedian called Noel Fielding, alongside doing shifts on an outsourced property section for the London *Evening Standard*. I lived from overdraft to panicked credit-card minimum-amount repayment, so although I read Michael Winner's column hungrily, my own dinner was often a jar of salty bottle-green pesto with a dusty lid from the corner shop stirred into cheap fusilli.

It was that sort of pesto, made of oil, dried basil and E-numbers, that stayed put on my thighs for months on end, forming a shimmering layer of trans-fat cellulite. I ate dinners of toast – made with the last of the frozen bread – with Marmite for the main course and lemon curd for the pudding. I ate it on my single bed, avoiding my housemate and his new girlfriend, who were conspiring to move me out and her in. Often after the toast I fell asleep without washing a shirt or in fact doing any laundry *again*, for the second week running, and would need to go to work without knickers, feeling not like a real woman but more like a feral animal. None of these things happened to the girls from *Marie Claire*. Their lives were 100 per cent perfect and I was going to become one of them.

'It's funny,' says one of the junior writers after I've been at *Marie Claire* on work experience for four weeks – two more weeks than scheduled – my overdraft and credit card groaning and swelling, my rent day looming. 'Your name is so long and grand,' she says. 'And then you actually see you.'

'Yes,' I laugh, leaving it hanging in the air. 'And then what happens?'

'Well, you begin talking and you're, well …' She pauses to find the word.

'What?' I say, raising an eyebrow.

'You're you,' she says.

'Hahahahaha, yes,' I laugh. She means common; I let this slide over me.

I'm pretty sure I only got through the doors at *Marie Claire* on unpaid work experience due to the use of my middle name, Georgina. Grace Georgina Dent. The Georgina, obviously, after my dad, George. This lengthened the short Northern fishwife grunt of Grace Dent and made it sound posher. I'd fooled them. And now I was in, like knotweed, taking root.

'So there's an editorial assistant job coming up?' I say.

'Yah,' she says as we wait at the fax machine. 'But they're still waiting to see if Chris and Lavender Patten's daughter is coming home from Hong Kong.'

'I see,' I say.

I could not afford to work for free. Nor did I give two hoots about *Marie Claire*'s output, which consisted of serious features like 'Avon ladies of the Amazon' and fashion spreads where a fourteen-year-old model from Denmark would be flown to Rio de Janeiro to stand in a favela and model £600 hot pants. But the lifestyle was certainly glamorous. It was intoxicating. I was the envy of everyone I knew from university. They were doing boring graduate training schemes for British Telecom; I was having fun at *Marie Claire*, doing the lunch run for beauty editors who just that morning had been on breakfast TV discussing armpit Botox. This was the new age of the ridiculously hip artisan sandwich: each day a delicatessen faxed a menu to the *Marie Claire* office, and I would ferry it back to the editorial floor and read it out loud in my Italian accent that I'd learned mainly from Dolmio adverts.

'Ahem ... focaccia al rosmarino, stracciatella and marinated Egyptian luffa, £3.95. Alsatian tarte flambée with leaves, £4. Organic pistou rustique with fougasse, £3.50!'

After announcing the menu, the assorted editors and sub-editors would wrinkle their noses and say, 'Ugh, not focaccia, I had my fill of that in Tuscany,' before stalking off to commandeer their table at the canteen, which they all hated.

I needed to shapeshift from being an anonymous, loitering, dispensable presence known to staff as 'the Workie' into something they saw as a payable human. *The Workie* – few people in Nineties media bothered to spare Generation X's feelings with terms like intern or job shadowing.

'So, this Patten girl?' I say.

'Yah, sweet thing. Tabitha is friends with her mother,' says the woman.

'Oh,' I say.

'How long are you here?' she asks, but it isn't a genuine question. No one in glossy magazines listens with both ears to the work experience girls.

'Not sure at the moment,' I say. 'I've got things to sort out.'

At *Marie Claire*, the unpaid fashion work experience girls were called, without even a wince, 'the cupboard people'. These young hopefuls lived for months on end in a small room with no windows at the back of the editorial floor filled with rails and rails of sample-size items. From 9 a.m. until 7 p.m. they telephoned stockists, called in garments from fashion houses, spoke to foreign embassies, stuffed clothes into suitcases and lugged suitcases up and down stairs.

'Where are my suitcases for Ghana? *Where are the cupboard people?*' the fashion editors would roar, stomping into the cupboard.

'I'm shooting with Testino on Saturday. Have they had all my customs waivers signed off by the embassy?'

Glossy magazine editors in the Nineties were accustomed to being a terrifically important deal. Within a decade or so this world would implode, killed by the Internet, their influence nigh-on decimated. Magazines would be bought mainly by hair salons to give customers something to look at when their stylist was hungover. But at one point, these people were gods. Their behaviour was legendary.

'You can't slap Taffeta, even if she really deserves it,' Clare told me on the first week of Workiedom – she was now working there too.

'She stood at my desk and stamped her feet like a little pony when I wouldn't drop all other jobs and ring a dispatch bike for her.'

'I'm not saying she doesn't deserve a slap,' Clare said. 'But her dad is much richer than yours, so she will have much better legal representation.'

Clare's words would ring in my ears many, many, many times over the next twenty years.

Despite all this, I wanted to stay at *Marie Claire*. I rather enjoyed these London high-society girls' whims and weirdnesses. Their lack of touchy-feeliness suited me; unabashed Nineties bitches were far easier to navigate than today's duplicitous blowhards staging elaborate Women's Day events and presenting as living saints with one eye on an OBE.

Not a jot of writing would be involved as editorial assistant. It was a secretarial dogs-body job. My desk would be right by the front door and referred to by the fashion department as 'reception'. However, if I got it, my name would go on the Who's Who list in the opening pages of the magazine, known as the masthead.

Grace Georgina Dent – Editorial Assistant.

I would also get paid about £13k per annum, which would allow me to pay rent and move to Camden Town, where I would, I planned, meet Malcolm McLaren, become his muse and forge a path to my role as a national treasure. There was definitely a job going here as dozens of CVs were beginning to arrive from posh girls with double-barrelled names and covering letters name-checking their fathers. As I stood by the shredder feeding them in, watching them turn to piles of ribbons, I knew one thing for sure: none of them were having it. The year before New Labour had swept to power making the D:Ream song 'Things Can Only Get Better' their anthem, and its title had become something of a mantra among the well-off metropolitan media set. I used to laugh when I heard them say this, because I'd known Currock, then Scotland, then the media world, and I thought, Well, literally how could life be any better than this?

October 1999

Flying first class for the first time, at the age of twenty-six, ruined me.

Absolutely ruined me.

It was as though a structural change happened to my DNA in mid-air, undoing centuries of lowborn family ancestry and topping me up with regal genes.

I had no idea life could be so fabulous. Until then, I didn't realise travelling could even be pleasant.

At Gatwick, as I boarded the flight, trip-trapping up the plane steps, I experienced something magical. I turned left at the top of the steps. Left. I entered a whole new cosmiverse called Club World. The air hostesses called me madam, ushered me to my seat and fetched a small, cold glass of champagne on a tray, with a paper-doily coaster. Then, an actual menu. Today's lunch would be salad Niçoise, then baked ravioli, chocolate torte and Brie de Meaux with port. A stiff grey curtain was then pulled across to separate me from standard-class hoi polloi. This was so that first-class people didn't have to look at everyday folks wearing loose-fitting travel garments with their bumbags, munching on big Toblerones. My first ten minutes behind the big curtain was already nicer than any actual holiday I'd been on. It was a long way from my first foreign excursion: the Dent family's package holiday by coach to Spain in the late Eighties. This getaway began with a thirty-six-hour coach ride from Carlisle Civic Centre, heading south via London, then to Calais before making a long trek to Catalonia. As I sat in first class with British Airways hostesses spooning treats into my lap as if I were a petulant baby starling, I thought about the shabby coach to Santa Susanna with the overflowing loo and the onboard 'snack bar', which was mainly supermarket-brand cup noodles and cans of warm Top Deck. The onboard enter-tainment was a single sixteen-inch TV screen playing *Smokey and the Bandit* on a loop. We arrived in Spain fed up, with swollen ankles and constipation.

First-class travel was not like that. I tottered down the plane's staircase in Austria feeling like a more special class of human being entirely. Even the most tub-thumping class warrior would find it hard to turn down their return ticket home. No one has ever, ever, ever left the upper-class side of an airplane thinking, that was nice, but I like sitting right at the back by the loo, getting my funny bone smacked by the perfume trolley.

After passport control, on a cold spring lunchtime in Austria, on my first official trip as editorial assistant at *Marie Claire*, I walked nervously towards the arrivals gate, pulling a small, cheap suitcase with a wonky wheel. I'd been sent to Vienna. I wasn't really sure why. Or even really where Vienna was. Aside from hearing Midge Ure scream about the place on *Top of the Pops* in the Eighties, I knew no real facts about the place. It meant nothing to me. However, as I walked through the arrivals gate I saw something else I'll never, ever get sick of: a smartly dressed man clutching a small white board with my name on it.

Miss Grace Georgiana-Bente.

OK, not my actual name. But he did mean me.

As hundreds of fellow travellers struggled with bags, searching for their connecting bus or train, Lukas swept the suitcase from my hand and walked me to his Mercedes-Benz, where a copy of American *Vogue* and a small glass bottle of gently carbonated Badoit Eau de Minérale sat in the armrest.

'You here for the conference, Miss Bente?' he said as we began our route to central Vienna.

'Ummmm, yes,' I said, hoping he'd not ask about any specifics.

'You are doctor – sorry, oncologist?' he said.

'Oh no, not an oncologist,' I said. 'I'm a writer.'

'Ah, writer, excellent, good,' he said, as if this was just as good.

I was not really there to write anything. This was a freebie. In glossy magazines the freebies were abundant. At *Eva* magazine the only things I'd been sent for free were 'women's neck massagers'. At *Marie Claire*, the freebies were much classier. We were knee-deep in free luxury leave-in conditioner, designer boar-bristle tangle combs, nail-strengthening vitamins and eye caviar. Oh, and flowers, never-ending flowers.

'Will someone take these vile Blushing Bride canna lilies that McQueen sent and give them to a hospice?' my favourite fashion editor Liz would shriek as I whisked away the offending bouquet – about 300 quid's worth – and left it out by the toilets. All this excess had probably begun to change me a bit. I was definitely not ringing Mam and Dad as much. With my job now permanent and my life faster and more glamorous, I was getting bad at keeping in touch with Clare too. She had left *Marie Claire* and gone to work on a special project in a different magazine house. We'd been missing each other's calls. And now I was distracted by a trip to Vienna.

'Next weekend?' I said to Tilly, the managing editor.

'Yah, it's a pharmaceutical thing, they want some press bods out there,' she said.

This editor liked me a lot, as I could perform magic tricks like 'retrieve a Chanel jacket from one of London's fanciest, grumpiest dry cleaners without the actual ticket' – a feat of

charm and bloody-mindedness that would earn me a round
of applause when I came back carrying the item.

'They can't teach that at Roedean,' she once said to me.

Stuff like this, and the lack of other good applications, is
possibly why I got the job.

So now here I was, one year into officially being Editorial
Assistant, checking in at the exceedingly grand Hotel Imperial,
Vienna, being escorted by the manager to one of their largest
suites for a two-night stay. He turned the key in the lock and
I squeaked with joy. This was an enormous apartment, with
a large sitting-room area, two bedrooms, many sofas and
decorative chaise longues and a glittering chandelier lighting
up the main room. This suite was at least three times the size
of the Dents' self-catering accommodation all those years ago
in Spain, where me and David had slept on pull-out beds.

I stood, mouth ajar, not quite listening as the manager
reminded me two, no, three, maybe four times that if I
required anything, literally anything, it would be his pleasure.
He left, moving backwards, sort of genuflecting as he closed
the door. I immediately flopped onto the super-king-sized bed
and lay in the middle, flailing my arms and legs out like an
octopus. Then I did some shots from a tray of the finest small-
batch schnapps, which was in a little glass jug on a tray on
the antique dressing table. I considered calling my old Brown
Owl from the phone beside the loo in the second bathroom
to tell her to shove her Sixer Badge up her arse, but it felt
petty, so instead I opened the handwritten letter from the
hotel manager, which came in a thick cream envelope with a

seal of soft red wax. This letter assured me – Miss Grace Georgina Bente – that I was an absolute priority. And should the merest hint of any whim that might accentuate my pleasure during this trip cross my mind over the next two days, I needed to contact him personally.

Day or night.

My needs would be top of their list, my pleasure was their one concern.

The entire staff of the hotel were waiting breathlessly for my call.

OK, this wasn't exactly what it said, but it was something equally as overblown, because this is how, I was learning of late, people spoke to you almost all of the time if they thought you were rich or important or useful to them.

You were a priority.

If you have ever noticed wealthy people boarding an easy-Jet flight looking flummoxed and ashen, this could be because they paid for Priority Boarding and then the Priority Boarding call-out didn't happen, and they complained and no one cared, and, well … it was a lot to take in. Maybe the greatest difference between being rich and poor is the number of instances per day that strangers inform you that you've been seen or your needs noted.

At this moment, I noticed a large set of doors on the far side of the room fastened by a large antique bolt. They seemed to lead somewhere. After some pulling and heaving, the bolt gave way and the doors clattered open to reveal a balcony! And there was the courtyard of the Vienna State Opera

House, lit ethereally as if prepared for a fairytale ball. I let out a shriek. It was quite simply the most beautiful view I had ever seen in real life. But quickly the joy felt bittersweet. To be all alone in this hotel room with this view felt a little bit sad. This room was priced at just short of £3,000 for a one-night stay. My family could never, ever experience it. This entire world was absolutely inaccessible to them. I tried to imagine them there: Dad on one of the sofas, with his slippers on, reading his newspaper. Mam giving the antique knick-knacks a onceover, saying, 'See that vase? Your Aunt Mildred had a bedpan that looked like that', and my brother Dave pouring us more schnapps.

For a millisecond I felt a little bit lonely. My London life was certainly gathering pace: I had a paid job that turned heads when it was mentioned at parties; I'd pitched some pieces to the *Guardian* via email and had the breakthrough of some 'try again, please' feedback. Better than that: I'd been put on some 'possible' lists to appear on late-night TV debate shows after getting my face in a few magazine spreads. They were always the kind of humiliating jobs all wannabe writers take at the start of their career to get exposure and live to regret. I appeared in *Marie Claire*'s health-and-beauty spin-off magazine holding rollerblades beside a totally made-up caption that said, 'I am devastated the body-doctor says my hourglass shape means I should give up blading or suffer thick thighs. It is my life and I can't imagine stopping.' My flatmates Eleanor and Craig had laughed until they were sick. Another time I was sent on a date with Sir Clive Sinclair to test what it was like to date a man with brains. He ditched me in the American Bar in the Savoy after one drink. This type of fame had led to semi-invites on the types of show where low-grade writers come on and shout a few things before the microphone moves on. TV fame. Now, I'd flown first class to Austria.

Why did I feel a tiny bit sad?

I imagined Clare spinning about on the balcony, saying, 'Grace, this is some serious Hans Christian Andersen nonsense.' Something had cooled between me and Clare, and it was totally my fault and I needed to address it. A few months before we'd had a silly run-in about a guestlist spot to a party – an ex-boyfriend of mine had taken a spot that was meant for me, and I was hurt, and she hadn't got that I was hurt, and we'd ended up bickering in the road outside IPC Magazines, but halfway through I'd jumped into a cab with the *Marie Claire* girls as I was late for a perfume launch, which now I thought about it was a little starry on my part. Her last words to me were, 'The thing with you, Grace, is that when you have been hurt it's like you go into witness protection. A wall goes up and then no one can reach you.' I'd thought as I got in the car that was very bloody astute. Maybe I should send Clare one of those SMS texts? Then a Public Relations girl called Jemima knocked on the door of my suite to tell me I had an hour to get ready before we all met in the lobby for champagne and I forgot all about London.

* * *

The Viennese trip – a weekend of non-stop eating, drinking and partying with surgeons and doctors in a luxury five-star hotel – was all paid for by a big pharmaceutical company. All I had to do in return for this splendid time drinking sturm and scoffing wiener schnitzel was hear the odd lecture about some research, pills and potions, and remember what nice people worked at this firm whenever I wrote about HRT, breast cancer or fertility problems. On the Sunday morning, when I woke up in a damp vintage Armand Basi frock after flinging myself into a hotel pool at 2 a.m. still clutching a bottle of Moët, I stared at the press releases for HRT pills strewn all over the carpet and thought, well, where is the harm in all this?

CHAPTER 6

BMW

February 2000

Although the Noughties sit hazily in my mind – with vast patches left unaccountable – I do recall clearly that as I left Bounds Green to move to a new rented flat in Putney, I packed up in such a hungover state that, absentmindedly, I shoved a number of the free 'women's neck massagers' from *Eva* magazine into the bag heading to the local charity shop. A day later, as the Man with a Van pulled away down the street, I noticed that one of the lovely old volunteer ladies who ran the shop had placed the most 'rabbity' one in the window, mistaking it for a ring tree. Events like this stand out. Also, around this time, I remember Piers Morgan, now editor of the *Daily Mirror*, standing outside his office on the twenty-second floor of the Canary Wharf tower yelling loudly to the entire newsroom, 'If any of you fucking lemmings leave this building to panic-buy petrol, you are fired!'

I bobbed my head out of sight and cackled. The chief sub-editor put his car keys down sheepishly. My time at the

Mirror started after an exodus of my favourite *Marie Claire* staffmembers shifted there to launch a free women's magazine called *M*, sweeping me along with them as a writer. My dad was properly proud when he found out. He'd been unimpressed by my other breakthrough around this time: writing some pop-culture pieces for the *Guardian*, which he believed was a communist rag only bought by social workers and do-gooders. The *Mirror*, on the other hand, was something he was proud to carry back from the newsagent.

After four years of relatively sedate magazine editorial floors, I found the constant racket of the *Mirror* newsroom comforting. It reminded me of the Dents' living room back in Carlisle where everybody shouted all the time, even when discussing simple things like who'd turn on the kettle. Piers Morgan as an editor was noisy, rambunctious, often hilarious and never, ever boring. He spent a lot of the time in an ongoing one-man argument, berating the world, often pulling other staff into the whirlwind. For the 1999 Christmas party, Morgan took the *M* girls to Marco Pierre White's Mirabelle, where Salman Rushdie came to the table to give his regards, Liz Hurley swept by, Joan Collins was in the house with Percy and I sat with my gob ajar. At least by now, despite being starstruck, I was much more prepared for a multitude of knives, forks and wine glasses.

'BMW', I'd taught myself. Bread, meal, wine: bread on the left, plate in the middle, wine on the right. But as Aunt Frieda says, after a few drinks no one cares. Furthermore, the posher the person, the less they cared about living by silly rules.

At the *Mirror* my desk was among the 3 a.m. Girls – a trio of infamous all-female gossip columnists – Jessica, Eva and Polly – who were currently causing havoc across celebrity land. As I sat at my keyboard typing up my latest world-changing article on dating trends, the 3 a.m. Girls' phonelines buzzed continuously with showbiz tittle-tattle, mainly about Kate Moss and the Primrose Hill set, who were having a fantastic time in north-west London. Although tabloid gossip in the Nineties and early Noughties was gleaned by some pretty nefarious means, little is often said about the large percentage of the dirt that came from celebrities' supposed friends. Or, at least, people the celebs believed were friends. Friendship in media London was nothing like everyday friendship. People ran hot and heavy with each other for a few months of parties, VIP rooms and summer yachting excursions, then moved on without a word to bigger, better things. Characters burned out and left London without warning or disappeared off the radar with no one caring enough to ask why. All this was a positive boon for gossip writers: there's nothing more lethal than a cohort or hanger-on who's been edged out of a glamorous gang. They tend to want money or revenge.

Reporting on famous people didn't interest me, but writing about real people did. Being twenty-seven, with no babies, no steady boyfriend and literally nothing to tie me down gave me freedom to jump on long-haul flights at a few hours' notice.

'Right, Grace, it's a waterpark in Hernando County in Tampa,' Marianne, the editor of *M*, would say. 'They have a daily mermaid display where local girls in fishtails swim about doing aquatic tricks. I need you to go and audition to be a mermaid.'

'But I'm not a brilliant swimmer,' I'd say.

'That makes it funnier!' she'd laugh. And by 5 p.m. I'd be in Boots at Heathrow Airport panic-buying a verruca sock. The weekend would be spent jetlagged wearing a spandex fishtail. The following weeks would feature a trip to the Bakken amusement park outside Copenhagen for the World Santa Claus Congress, where thousands of avuncular men dressed in red velour suits swapped tips on fake beards and dealing with advent grotto burnout. After that I was off to a nudist resort in Catalonia to play giant chess in the buff with a team of enthusiastic naked Germans.

Phone calls home to Mam and Dad back in boring old Carlisle began to grow further apart. Friends I'd had in my first months in London – Clare, the *Eva* team, my old uni crowd – fell by the wayside, replaced by fourteen-day American excursions to Miami and Upstate New York or to Negril in Jamaica, travelling with photographers who very often I'd met only for the first time at the airport before embarking on days of winging it, interviewing and photo-sessions in full Magenta Devine mode, before returning home to the UK to type it up through the night in my tiny box bedroom in Putney. Still, there are few things, I was starting to see, that are lonelier than pushing a trolley through the arrivals gate after a super-exciting foreign trip to find abso-lutely nobody at the airport to meet you; than no one caring that you're home safe as no one really noticed you'd gone. Because everyone has largely given up trying to keep track.

However, each time I appeared in the newspaper, something made up for any of these minor stabs of self-pity.

'Are you … that girl from the *Mirror*?' a woman asked me one morning on the Victoria Line.

'Yes, yes, I am,' I said.

'Oh good, I like you, you're very funny,' she said and walked off.

And there it was. At last. That feeling was terrific.

Strangers knew my name. It felt better than love. This was exactly the kind of fabulous, starry, spiritually cleansing incident I'd dreamed of when I sat in the Binns café with Darren and Caroline, thirteen years previously, under a pile of crimped hair reading out my minuscule *NME* debut. Soon, something even more triumphant appeared on the horizon. My first ever TV appearance: on a late-night regional debate show hosted by one of my heroes – a glamorous female football manageress called Karren Brady. The topical debate I was chipping in on was the heady topic of whether having sex with 100 people during a one-week package holiday in Kavos was really good for one's self-worth. Rather prudishly, I was arguing possibly not.

On the train to Nottingham to film the show, I felt bilious with fright. My new slimming obsession, the Atkins Diet, wasn't helping. One solitary boiled egg for breakfast, then black coffee for lunch and dinner with occasional pieces of grilled chicken had indeed given me a size-ten body and cheekbones like razors, but I also had breath like Satan's bumcleft and the occasional minor blackout. Importantly, though, I was camera-ready, as they say in showbusiness – which means suitable at a given moment to slot into a TV show. This actually means twelve pounds under your body's natural resting weight and with a haircut that costs at least £100 a trim. I was camera-ready to meet Karren Brady, and at midnight I sat on the front row of the audience feeling hot and bilious, repeating inside my head the two clever lines that I was determined to say regardless of whatever question was asked. As the camera panned towards me, somehow, in some manner, I stuttered them out. At least, I think I did. I made a noise, for sure, and received some sort of minor applause from those around me. I floated into the green room afterwards as high as a kite. I had been on live television, for thirty-three seconds, after midnight, on a channel that broadcasted mainly to Nottingham. More people would have seen me on CCTV if I'd been shoplifting in ASDA.

Still, I was a television star.

The doors to heaven had been flung open wide.

March 2000

Despite now being a bona fide Z-list celebrity and international jetsetter, there was one genre of journalist invitation that instilled fear in me. Gastronomical extravaganzas, where the crowd would be mainly food or wine experts – such as a

trip I was offered to Paris to celebrate the opening of a spec-
tacular new wine cellar, featuring an overnight stay at the
luxurious, totally unmissable George V hotel just off the
Champs-Élysées. The guestlist was a crowd of wine experts
from trade magazines; there were a lot of Huberts, Pierres
and Hectors. After RSVPing yes, I fretted for days about the
decision. The way people acted around fine wines and wine
lists was terrifying. It felt like a secret language requiring
decades of experience, rooted in childhood, which I could
never catch up on. Before leaving my grand hotel suite on the
Friday evening to meet the group, I necked a shot of Drambuie
for courage. Waiting for me in the lobby was a group of rather
well-upholstered men from the Home Counties with wry
smiles, red veins sweeping up from their noses and wispy
eyebrows. There were also two women with straight, mousy
hair; one had a velour Alice band, the other seemed to be
called Boudica. In the twinkling lobby they swapped anec-
dotes about recent trips to the Napa Valley, Languedoc-
Roussillon and Patagonia. They name-checked specific
vineyards, soil slopes, water run-offs and mineral levels, and
debated the arguments for and against traditional *Quercus
robur* barrels. I wanted the floor to swallow me up.

As we took our places at the magnificent table, a myriad of
staff began to flap about making everything perfect, as they
always do when the table is full of journalists. Why did I
come on this trip? I asked myself. My fleeting knowledge of
Jacob's Creek Shiraz would only stretch so far before the
truth was known that I was, beneath all the swagger, just a

gap-toothed Eliza Doolittle. At any point the sommelier was bound to ask me to choose wine for the table, forcing me to flap through his multi-paged laminated hellscape of un-pronounceable names. As Hector – resplendent in a tweed waistcoat and natty bowtie – took the chair beside me and the waiter tucked him in, I closed my eyes and regained my composure. Then the hell inside my head began to be enacted in real life.

'Madame,' said the sommelier, 'would you care to choose some wine for the table?'

He was brandishing a thick, hardbacked book.

'UghghghghdoIhaveto?' I said

'I beg your pardon?' he said, craning to hear.

The entire table stopped talking. They gazed at me, then at the sommelier's voluminous tome, then back at me.

Mercifully, at this point, a hero jumped in and saved me.

'I'll take that,' said Hector, with a wink.

'Sir,' nodded the sommelier, handing it to him.

'So what are we thinking ... what are we eating?' said Hector casually, as if talking to no one in particular, and in the blink of an eye the sommelier sprang to life, rabbiting on about bottles he had taken the liberty of 'allowing to breathe' and other rare ones he hoped we'd be kind enough to taste.

'So, you don't like choosing wine?' Hector said quietly after the sommelier had left.

I opted to come clean. I had nothing to lose. I knew rela-tively nothing about wine. I'd only come on this trip for a night in a fine hotel in Paris and to stock up on mascaras in the big Sephora. I thanked Hector for stepping in before I tried to choose an affordable red, mistakenly ordered something rare worth 10,000 francs and had my passport confiscated by gendarmerie.

'Well, tell the sommelier when he arrives that you don't want to spend a lot and ask what he recommends.' Hector laughed.

'But then he'll want to talk to me,' I blushed.

'Oh, he doesn't want to talk to you,' Hector said. 'He wants to talk at you. It's just a game. The sommelier's job is to know everything about the bottles on the list. Your only job is to drink it. The winning tactic,' he continued, 'is to seem genuinely interested when they harp on. It's simple, really.'

'But ... what about when they pour some?' I said. 'What do I say then?'

'Again, very little,' he said.

He mimed the act of picking up the glass by the stem, staring for a second at the colour, stuffing his nose in it for a small sniff and letting the barest amount enter his mouth.

'Good,' he said.

'Is that all I say? Good,' I said.

'Well, you're not tasting for flavour, you're checking it's not off, which it won't be,' he said. My head was spinning by now.

'OK, but what if I look in the book and it's all really expensive?' I asked. 'What do I say then?'

'Oh ... OK, here is what I would do,' he said. He beckoned the sommelier over in a very blasé fashion.

'Incidentally, what are the house wines? If we make this a long night,' he said. 'Are they drinkable?'

This question was miraculous.

Hector was saying 'we want the cheapest bottle you possess', but instead of the sommelier sneering at us, he began justifying why these wines were the cleverest choices on the list – they were his own personal choices. So versatile, so pocket-friendly. He and his staff drank this themselves after-hours.

'We'll have two of each later on,' said Hector.

I'd learned enough about wine in eleven short minutes to prepare me for a lifetime.

Weeks later, I chose wine for the table at The Ritz Carlton in Montreal on a trip with the son of a prominent Tory MP and the exceedingly posh brother of a New York It girl who had one of those second names that make conversations stop and people crane forwards. Over three nights I developed a liking for vintage Armagnac and ate my very first truffle, plucked from Montferrato woodland crevices and grated over *oeufs cocotte* each morning. It tasted oddly of unwashed feet, if I'm honest. I also unknowingly ate my first foie gras, which the boys thought was very funny as they reminded me which part of the goose this actually was and how it was extracted.

'I just think for the amount they torture the goose,' I cried, 'it might taste less like meaty snot!'

A few weeks after that, I flew to Israel first class to be whisked around Eilat's most elegant and artsy boutique hotels, before a dreamy sojourn at a Dead Sea spa resort hotel, where I floated in the salt lake and was fed kubeh, chraime and knafeh by Israeli tourist-board officials as they told me what a bright utopia the place was for each and every one of the residents. These trips were completely free. Or at least they came with secret price tags: a glowing travel piece here, a glowing review for a duff movie or atrocious perfume there. Yet, with each trip to a far-off place, the etiquette of dealing with fancy living became less opaque. It was not any of the stuff I'd read as a little girl in those 'Dos and Don'ts' lists they'd print from time to time in the paper, advising women to walk with books on our heads to achieve refined posture. Nor was it merely saying 'Sorry?' instead of 'Yerwhat?' No, the rules of sneaking into upper-class spaces and passing as posh were much more nuanced; it was a spurious cocktail of bluffing and well-timed name-dropping, mixed with an air of pseudo-effortless confidence and sometimes, when faced with someone who was trying to impress you, giving almost no reaction at all.

In early March 2000, I landed at Dulles International Airport and walked through arrivals, pulling my Samsonite suitcase, checking my missed calls on my Nokia, but opting not to bother picking up the voicemails as I was absolutely too busy and possibly more than a little full of myself. I'd had my face on TV a bit more that week on a BBC Two show about Eighties nostalgia, plus a tentative offer of a book deal to write children's fiction. Plus, here I was, in Washington, DC, about to go straight out for dinner with a long-distance boyfriend I'd met on a job in the Caribbean. As we drove out of the car park, I noticed another missed call from Nicole, an old *Marie Claire* friend, which I was much too busy to take, and I ignored other calls as I arrived at Martin's Tavern, a bar and grill, for cocktails. I ignored those bleeps and buzzes for a while longer, but after my first very strong dry martini with an olive, I deigned to pop outside into the fresh DC evening air and listen to these messages from people who were very probably trying to get me to write for them, what with me being a rising star. The very first message was from Nicole. She said, 'I know this is a shock, but it's about Clare. She didn't tell many people she was ill, but, Grace, over the last year she's had ovarian cancer and, well, it was all very quick. We were trying to get you, but anyway, she went home to her mum's up north and ... well, here's the thing, she's died. But she wanted you to know this one thing: the summer you all ran rampage across London was one of the best times in her whole life.'

I sat down on a nearby wall and I opened my mouth and I howled.

CHAPTER 7

Limitless Gravy

March 2008

In a booth decorated with a framed photo of Sid James in *Carry On Camping*, I'm having an early dinner with Mam and Dad. We're in their favourite restaurant, the Toby Carvery, Carlisle, just off Junction 43 on the M6. In the eight years since Clare died, I've thought many times how much she'd have enjoyed my various victories in my route to small-time fame and fortune. She'd have loved seeing my face cropping up constantly on TV, sometimes three times per night, on shows with names like *Britain's Favourite Biscuit* on Channel 5 and then, hours later, on *Newsnight Review* on BBC Two discussing Ingmar Bergman. Clare would have rolled her eyes at my ability to sit on a chair with a camera on my face and have opinions on almost any given subject – Space Hoppers, Scottish devolution, the Backstreet Boys – as long as there was a little money involved. She'd have definitely enjoyed seeing me promoting my string of Young Adult novels, which led to me giving readings and small motivational talks in schools all over Britain – although my own former secondary school were peculiarly unkeen to hear my memories. She'd have seen me begin writing a TV column for the *Guardian*, appearing on Radio 1 doing book reviews and starting to use my lilting regional accent for voiceovers. But best of all, me and her would have been able to drink wine together around the kitchen table in my little house in East London, the one I put a down payment on using the proceeds of all these things. Also, along the way, I'd met a man – a record executive – fallen madly in love, eloped to America and got married. It rankled me quietly that Clare and I had bickered over some boy who felt so important to me at the time yet who had now faded to that level of importance where I wouldn't care if he bumped into me in the Spar when I was wearing my dressing gown.

It's 4 p.m. at the Toby Carvery. Now that they're retired, Mam and Dad like to have their teas out early. Sometimes fish and chips in the Morrisons' café or a jacket spud in a local garden centre. Lately, though, their hearts have belonged firmly to the Toby.

'I'll have a glass of Shiraz,' Dad says to the waitress. 'Jacob's Creek,' he winks to me. 'Australian.'

Dad knew very few facts about wine, but he delivered them with great certainty – not unlike your average Islington dinner-party wine buff. As Dad aged (he was now just past seventy), wild silver shoots began to fire from his jet-black hair at tangential angles. Mam nicknamed him 'Frowsy Freddy' and spent a lot of her time handing him a comb and nagging him to put on a nicer jersey.

'He'll wear the same thing for days,' she would complain. 'It's like he's determined to look like a tramp.'

My parents had sold the family house, Mam having drastically devalued it with a heady blend of pebble dash, breeze blocks and Artex swirls. They moved to a small retirement flat on the opposite side of Carlisle, cramming the same number of ornaments, mock-Victorian knick-knacks and horse brass into an eighth of the space. Dingley Dell, I call it, preferring to live in a minimalist Scandi-influenced space where the lounge contains one slate-coloured sofa facing a television and some artily arranged books. The only way to keep this minimal space tidy is to shred every piece of household paperwork as it appears and hover vigilantly with a Muji lint roller, removing bobbles and random cat hairs from the citrus-coloured Habitat pouffe as they land.

'OK,' I say, recapping on the etiquette. 'I can go back to the vegetable section as many times as I want?'

'Yes,' Mam says.

'But I can go to the meat section only once?' I say, glancing over at a man in chef's whites slicing at a ginormous turkey crown.

It could feasibly be emu. You could imagine Rod Hull chasing Michael Parkinson with it hooked over his arm. Why am I eating here?

I've lived in London for about twelve years and have sweet-talked and sharp-elbowed my way into some of the capital's strangest concept restaurants, but none of them have been quite like Toby's. The walls are covered with photos of British comedy classics: Mr Bean is playing golf and there's a young Jim Davidson. Beside the turkey is a honking lump of very well-cooked beef. Not a scrap of blood left in it. Then a large slab of mystery meat that Dad assures me is roast pork.

'What's the turkey like?' I ask.

'Bit dry,' says Mam. 'But there's gravy over there. As much as you want.'

I've had it drilled into me by now by London's polite society that the word 'gravy' is frowned upon. The word is *jus*. And it should be used sparingly. It should not be applied with a ladle in proportions one could paddle in.

As a French photographer on a glossy mag shoot once said to me, 'Why would you make zomething to make the meat less dry? Why not you English just make the meat less dry when you cook? Why are you admitting defeat before you begin cooking?'

I stare at the gravy station with its communal ladles and slightly sticky jugs.

'George, look at her face, look at it!' laughs Mam. 'It's four quid for the carvery! Four! You can't turn your nose up at that price. Oh, she's too posh for this now. Too posh!'

Dad shakes his head and heads off to collect his plate.

The longer I lived in London, the further the gap grew between my tastes and theirs. And the more bewildered they were by my life choices. They were politely bewildered by my choice to get married in Vegas, wearing a forty-quid Laura Ashley tea frock, using witnesses we found on the day. I thought it was highly romantic. Like Demi and Bruce, like

Don Johnson and Melanie Griffiths! They were bewildered by my and my husband's choice to set up home in East London – no place to bring up kids – and then refuse to fit carpets.

'Can you not afford carpet just now?' Mam said.

'The floorboards are polished,' I told them. 'Look, I've had them *restored*.'

'Nice bit of shag pile would make the place feel like a home,' Dad said.

'I don't want carpets,' I huffed.

'Oh, it's *posh*, George, leave her,' Mam said.

By 2008 I was rather high on the coup of being a presenter on lofty high-brow arts programme *The Culture Show* on BBC Two: my most Paula Yates moment to date. I was given my own make-up artist called Kevin, who was a miracle worker, and before the series began I'd been whisked off for champagne at the Groucho by a BBC controller in order to be told effusively what a fantastic gift I was to modern television. I was feeling pretty pleased with myself. Obviously, Mam was standing for none of this, especially down Toby's.

'The vegetables look like they've just been tipped out of a freezer bag into a tray by someone on day release,' I say.

'It's four quid for as much as you can eat,' she says. 'You can't knock it, can you? Anyway, they freeze veg when it's fresh.'

I could never convince my family when I talked about eating out that paying four pounds for a small side dish of *pommes boulangère* was worth it because these potatoes were not only from a local smallholding, they'd also been scrubbed, scraped, sliced thinly by trained, salaried chefs, ladled with excellent-quality beef stock, organic full-cream milk and home-pressed olive oil and placed carefully in an oven for fifty minutes. This was *why* they were four quid.

'Four quid for a bowl of potatoes, on top of your main dish?' Mam would laugh. 'That is ridiculous.'

By now I was moving in circles with people who believed that the true goal of eating should be to taste great food, rather than simply be full.

And obviously I agreed. Or at least I made the right sounds. But deep down I knew this wasn't the case.

Not always, anyway.

Eating really is not that clear cut.

Sometimes it is lovely to eat and eat and eat, letting things that are perhaps only just semi-nice slide down your throat, until you end up incredibly full and even a little sore. The dirty truth about eating is that sometimes nothing is lovelier than starting a packet of Jaffa Cakes when you're feeling a little blue, eating two, maybe three, then finishing the entire packet. Sometimes my favourite dinner of all, when I'd had a shit day and my husband was out, was a bowl of McCain oven chips with a jug of Bisto powdered gravy and mint sauce. I kept this kind of thing quiet now that I was the sort of person who might share a backstage yurt at Hay-on-Wye with Alan Yentob.

David, my younger brother, found my ideas of grandeur deeply entertaining. He kept them in check with great glee. On this particular 'flying visit' up north – one of the two short trips I'd deigned to grant my family that year – I'd swaggered off the train from Euston in a silver, slightly fluffy Max Mara belted coat worth £800, only to find he'd forgotten to pick me up.

After I'd spent twenty minutes fuming outside the station, David appeared in his Audi with twelve pounds of King Edward potatoes in the front seat and his daughter Lola howling in a car seat in the back. Dave had met a nice Scouse girl called Tam, got married and had a little girl. He had grown up so much – in some ways.

'All right, face-ache! 'Ere, I like your coat. You're like one of the Wombles,' he said.

'Cheers,' I said.

'Gerrin, you'll have to stick the spuds on your knee,' he said.

As we drove through Carlisle to Mam and Dad's flat, I talked laboriously at him about a new, erudite BBC Two show called *Screenwipe* I'd been filming for a *Guardian* colleague called Charlie Brooker. It was getting terrific hype in all the places that mattered.

'Tell you what show you'd be good on,' Dave butted in.

'Go on.'

'Have you seen *Hole in the Wall*?' he said. 'It's on BBC One. There's this swimming pool, right, and this moving wall coming towards it. You have to jump through the hole as the wall comes for you.'

'The one where the players wear tight silver boiler suits?' I said.

'That's it!'

'I'm not going on *Hole in the Wall*, David,' I said.

'This is the problem with you nowadays,' he laughs. 'You'd have loved that wall if it had been down Rhyl Sun Centre. You're too posh now.'

Was I posh now?

As I sat in the Toby Carvery eating my emu and giant Yorkshire pudding, I began to wonder.

Posh was a word I heard a lot as a kid.

It was usually an accusation.

Mrs Allen at Number 9 was posh because she wouldn't let her kids play with me and David. They weren't allowed to eat biscuits in the street or hang about the lamppost like we were. *Pgh*, posh. Aunt Frieda did posh things; she played bridge and sometimes wore a wax jacket. By these standards, yes, I was posh. I'd changed. I was verging on grand.

Certainly, after years away, I now knew that none of the posh people I'd known up north were really, genuinely wealthy. In London, I'd discovered a whole new class of people living their lives in a way I'd never dreamed of previously. Properly, properly posh.

Until I got to London I'd never known anyone like my friend Luke, who'd been handed a multi-million-pound flat in South Kensington by an elderly relative legally swerving inheritance tax. Or anyone like my friend Cara, whose family had a spare unused family mansion on the Isle of Wight because they preferred to do Christmas in their second home – a farmhouse in the Cotswolds. I'd never met anyone like my beauty-editor friend Pascal, who threw her mother a birthday garden party in a Juan-les-Pins meadow in Antibes, featuring a live New Orleans jazz band and local dignitaries and CEOs of fashion houses as guests. This is posh. Posh is having so much money subliminally available, floating about in the ether via forthcoming inheritances, that you couldn't understand being working class if you tried. I was certainly not that. I could never be that: that sort of wealth is handed down.

Still, I definitely had more money. That was an irrefutable truth. Royalty cheques from my books were coming in from America and all over Europe. And I loved the way they felt in my bank account, sitting there like a comfort blanket. I'd been told many times during my life that money doesn't make you happy, but in recent years I'd started to wonder if this was not a huge hoax created by the ruling class to stop povvos like me asking for it. Because although money didn't make people happier, it certainly made everything easier. Everything. I was happy to never root through the reduced stickers in Iceland when the cash machine would only give me a five-quid note. I was happy when I used a private doctor working out of Soho rather than waiting nine working days for an NHS appointment to beg for a course of antibiotics. I was happy when I got in cabs and never had to run the last terrifying half-mile from the night bus to home. Every cheque that appeared in my account made me happy. And sometimes I liked to spend them on stupid things like coats that made me look like Madame Cholet from *The Wombles*.

Maybe all this meant I was now middle class?

No.

Never.

Nobody with silver fillings like mine and no maths GCSE is middle class.

'Go on, have a pudding, they're good,' says my mam.

'Have a pudding, presh, go on,' my dad says. 'I'm having the chocolate fudge cake.'

'*Dad*, you're not meant to be having ...' I begin, but my mother rolls her eyes as if to say, don't waste your time.

I want to harangue my father over his diabetes and the wisdom of ordering chocolate cake served with ice cream and thick chocolate drizzle, but as ever I know he'd wear us into silence.

Why spoil a nice time with an argument?

What can I change anyway? I don't live here.

And when I look back now, I realise some of the happiest times I ever had with Mam and Dad were down at Toby's, drinking Oscar Bay Merlot, eating carvery and laughing.

'OK ...' I say, scanning the menu. 'I'll have the cookie-dough sundae.'

They both smile.

They're never happier with me than when I am eating.

November 2008

It is Thursday, mid-morning, in my small, very messy home office. A clean desk is a symbol of an empty mind, I tell myself as I sit among the rubble of tattered notepads, spider charts that plan my latest column, press releases, discarded false eyelashes that look like dying spiders and coffee cups. A framed photo of Cleo Rocos on *The Kenny Everett Show* in stockings and suspenders smiles down at me. I'm supposed to be writing the opening paragraph of a *Guardian* column. Instead, I have my iPhone clamped between my shoulder and my ear joining a switchboard queue for a hot new restaurant. I'm hiding from a growing reality in my world that I feel I'm the first person to work out.

But restaurants are a wonderful distraction, and everyone is talking about this one. It's a glitzy new modern Russian brasserie in the heart of Soho named Bob Bob Ricard. It has quirky 'Press for Champagne' buttons in each booth to summon the waiting staff with elegant coupes of Pol Roger at a moment's notice. It serves fancy chicken Kiev for around £18, caviar with blinis and iced vodka shots. It has a huge buzz.

Everyone wants to go.

After living in London for twelve years, I know the unwritten rules of how to squeeze my bottom past the queue in its opening weeks. This involves a type of grubby psychological warfare. It requires name-dropping, plea-bargaining and obsequious grovelling. If it's done properly, one should feel thoroughly ashamed of oneself afterwards but filthily excited too. You've done it. You're in.

The hottest, most talked-about food in Britain is actually only accessible to about 0.1 per cent of its population. Everyone else has to go to Café Rouge.

Or Toby's.

As I wait, a yellow Post-it note on the side of my computer says: 'Call Dad's GP – make aware about all the stuff.'

I wrote this note to myself as a reminder.

But now it's reminding me and it feels painful, so I tear it off and place it face-down in order to continue the game at hand.

I'm like a terrier about getting into a good restaurant. I began honing my skills in 1998 at a place called Moro. Very hot. Very buzzy. Moro in Exmouth Market in Islington – New Labour territory – was the coolest place on earth. It served this brand-new thing called Moorish cuisine. Yes, I'm sure the North African Muslims occupying Spain in the eighth century may have quibbled with this, but the only moors most Brits had a working knowledge of at this point were in the Peak District.

Moro was one of those places that *everyone* was suddenly talking about. I mean everyone: the features desk at *The Face*, Michael Winner, Jay Kay from Jamiroquai, the researchers on *MasterChef* 1998 and the folk who high-fived Chris Evans as he walked past to get into the bar on *TFI Friday*. *Everyone*. I was already dropping Moro facts casually into conversation. 'Ummm, yes, they put a drop of orange oil in their flatbread, y'know?' Getting a table would be difficult. But who knew, if I mastered this, maybe then I'd chance my arm at other trendy places, such as Damien Hirst's Pharmacy, where I longed to perch on a pill-shaped bar stool and sip a cough-syrup cocktail beside strategically stacked piles of haemorrhoid-cream packets. Or even stray behind the velvet rope at Oliver Peyton's Atlantic Bar & Grill to eat Caesar salad with Gary from Reef and Natalie Imbruglia.

London was so exciting. No wonder I got lost here for so many years.

'When, sorry?' said the voice when Moro's reservation desk picked up.

'S ... S ... Saturday... this ... er ... weekend, please,' I stuttered.

'*Caghh,*' was the exact sound the woman made.

It wasn't a laugh, more a splutter of breath that seemed to say, '*You must be out of your mind.*'

'Nothing all weekend, sorry,' she said and then the phone went dead.

It was that sort of front-of-house rude that doesn't feel rude immediately. But then it does and it increases the more you think about it. Then it feels like you're wetting yourself in public.

'Well, I bet this doesn't happen to Michael Winner,' I blushed.

Then I was more determined to go than before.

Six weeks later, I called Moro again, pep-talked by my starry magazine friends. My elbows were ever so slightly sharper, my tone more demanding and clippily self-important. Somehow I managed to snare a midweek early table and invited the latest love of my life, Cliff, a newly qualified High Court barrister that I'd met in a Firkin pub near to closing time. The only thing we really had in common was that my friend was planning to have sex with his. Our relationship lasted two dates; my memories of Moro have lasted a lifetime.

Good restaurants change how you view eating forever. Moro was the start of me thinking a dressed small plate of cannellini white beans in oil and herbs was an actual reason to leave the house, rather than 'something you might eat during a siege'. I tasted my first harissa. I ate monkfish in sherry, then yoghurt and pistachio cake. Weirder still, dinner came in no proper order: small plates, big plates, just whenever the chef was ready. Mind-blowing. And not very filling. The barrister paid £80 for two of us and we both left hungry. So metropolitan! Only London people leave dinner unfazed by needing a round of toast afterwards.

But it's fun to be in there at the start of a new scene. Soon Moro's sumac-stained footprints were all over British gastropub menus; its recipes ripped off and reproduced on Saturday-morning telly. These trends trickled down.

OK, they never trickled down to the Toby Carvery, Carlisle.

Over the last year, Mam has confessed to me, Toby's has become almost the only place Dad will go. He no longer wants to book cruises. He'll go to Blackpool at a push as long as she always books the same hotel, and even then it makes him anxious. And to the local garage for his lottery ticket. It's as if almost everywhere unnerves him aside from his bedroom and his chair in the lounge. His world has become smaller and his habits more eccentric. He picked a fight with a neighbour for posting a church magazine through his letterbox. He seemed to believe it was something Satanic. He collected twenty pence pieces avidly in little plastic bags, then hid them under the bed. The last time me and him spoke in person, he told quite a detailed a story about a specific medical appointment. He told me about the examination, the prognosis. Afterwards Mam assured me this appointment didn't happen. We decided, together, after throwing the topic around and coming up with a reasonable excuse, that he must have got mixed up.

My call moves further in the Bob Bob Ricard queue.

I put all these things out of my mind.

Eventually my call is answered. I spring to life and know exactly how to get in. I use my name, which is vaguely recognisable from the telly and newspapers, and a smattering of sparkle about my record-industry husband and they give me a table for four at the time I want on a Saturday night. As ever, when I put the phone down I feel a little grubby and ashamed.

Why would I ever go back to Carlisle now that I'm a priority?

But like all daughters who run off chasing bigger, better things, I could hear a siren calling.

2009

'He's been hiding chocolate in me glory hole again,' Mam fumes down the phone. I place my hand over the receiver. Former children's TV presenter Andi Peters is having his face powdered in the make-up chair next to me. I explain to Mam again that the term 'glory hole' has shifted meaning in recent times. It no longer suggests a place to shove random bric-a-brac. It is Day 86 in the *Big Brother 10* house and I'm appearing on a Channel 4 Friday-night spin-off show to interview the twelfth housemate to be evicted. Live television. If you can pull off live TV, it's one of the sharpest thrills of all.

'Why do you have to be so filthy?' Mam says.

'I'm not being filthy!' I say. 'It doesn't mean cupboard anymore.'

Dad's fuzzy-headedness is definitely due to his diabetes. Mum, Dave and I have decided this. Mam has been trying, and failing, to keep tabs on his Dairy Milk intake again. This has been going badly. Dad's determination to eat Fruit & Nut by the square foot involves chutzpah similar to Steve McQueen's in *The Great Escape*. On trips to the garage to buy his *Daily Mail* and lottery ticket he's buying multiple bars of chocolate and sneaking them into the house up his jumper. He hides them inside a shoebox under a pile of old jumpers in the airing cupboard.

'What about his pills?' I ask. 'Are they under control?'

Dad has taken his Metformin strategically for many years. He uses it like magical fairy dust to counteract a full ASDA family-sized strawberry trifle. He hangs back on the pills when he's being good, then takes double when he's binged. We pretend – as it's easier all round – not to notice him slurring his words a little or not really knowing who I am when I call until I explain. Or when pins and needles began in his feet. Or when he falls asleep mid-conversation. In recent weeks I've finally gone behind Dad's back and called his doctor. But without any consent to discuss his medical problems, they fobbed me off quickly. I would need to get a health-and-welfare Lasting Power of Attorney form signed by him to give me any power to begin interfering properly. This feels like a big reach considering I've spent four decades letting him wriggle out of discussing his other children, or even apologising to me for an entire childhood of his fibbing.

The wardrobe mistress appears, delivering my newly ironed dark green dress and the soundman is trying to hang a microphone pack off my bra. We are going live on Channel 4 in forty-five minutes to a couple of million viewers. I don't have time to think about Carlisle.

'He left his credit card at the newsagent again today,' Mam says.

'Again?' I say.

'I know,' she says. 'It's like a fog descends on his brain.'

'Yes,' I say. The penny is beginning to drop.

* * *

In my dressing room, I chuck back a small glass of Chenin blanc while waiting to go on set, where the audience are being warmed up by a comedian telling the same warm-up jokes I've heard a dozen times before, but they're working. The audience is laughing. My best-friend Matt, a Public Relations boss, is reading me messages from my 20,000 followers on this amazing new ever-so-positive social-media wormhole called Twitter, where feedback from absolute strangers is instant. It's just an endless stream of people telling me they like me! This new social-media platform means everyone can contact anyone now. I've chatted to Simon Le Bon and Curt Smith from Tears for Fears. Everyone is so friendly; it almost seems too good to be true.

Shortly before the show goes live, a window fitter from Brentwood called Marcus Akin who dresses like Wolverine is evicted from the *Big Brother* house, spilling out of the famous doors, across the walkway, past the screaming crowds and eventually into the adjoining TV studio, where behind a desk Davina McCall, Andi Peters and I interrogate him on his behaviour. I hit most of my VTs and even get some big laughs and applause and then wander victoriously into the green-room booze-up full of TV researchers and evicted *Big Brother* contestants like Charlie and Karly and Dogface and Rodrigo and bottles of warm Blossom Hill plonk from Borehamwood Tesco Extra. Then into a chauffeured Mercedes-Benz, which whips me home down the M25, where, in our dark, quiet house, my husband has gone to bed. A pile of fan letters sits on the table, including a request to be the patron of a nearby donkey sanctuary and some weird fan art where someone has painted my face in crisp white Tipp-Ex. I give it a sniff. I don't think it's Tipp-Ex at all.

My husband does not get up to say hello. He didn't call to say he watched me. Maybe he's sick and tired of waiting for me while I hobnob with folk off the telly in green rooms and finding almost everything I need spiritually from appearing on TV in studios with bright lights and shiny floors. In our expensive designer fridge, the shelves are empty. I've left a Post-it note on the front, which says, 'Try Dad's doctor again.' A leftover slice of Domino's pizza sits in a box on the kitchen work surface. Decent wives do not let their husbands go to bed as they're hanging out in green rooms, I think quietly. Nor do they let their husbands order Domino's again. I feel guilty and know I should have left some sort of casserole. Food is how you show people you love them. I feel guilty when I admit to myself that such pre-historic ideas hold any scrap of veracity. I wish desperately it was untrue. Twitter says tonight I did great.

CHAPTER 8

Sex on the Beach

October 2009

Being a grown-up lady in her kitchen felt like so much fun when I was little. Standing at my Fisher-Price toy stove, prodding invisible bacon, pretending to be in charge, calling the shots, just like Mammy. But now I'm less enraptured. As my husband talks online with colleagues in Los Angeles, a rerun of *MasterChef: The Professionals* plays mutely in the corner of the room on one of the digital channels. The screen on our large TV is dusty. I'm standing in the kitchen, floundering. I promised to cook dinner tonight as part of a concerted effort to be a decent wife. A better wife. A long stare into the fridge achieves little. I had four meetings today about developing one of my Shiraz Bailey Wood novels into a movie, then a voice-over, which meant I missed my *Guardian* column deadline. I'll need to do it pre-dawn before I leave while also pulling together some tax details for my accountant. I have a 5 a.m. alarm set.

I have a migraine behind my right eye.

I also have: half a bag of organic baby leaf spinach going mushy, three farmers'-market eggs in a box, now of dubious vintage, and one onion with a long white sprout. My fingers dance towards my MacBook to begin browsing the website Just Eat. Then they stop. Good wives don't let their husband's dinner arrive via bike in a plastic box, even if he wouldn't judge me for it. He is very amenable about the fact that I have a career. Or maybe, a small voice inside says, I have worn him down to expect less. The second option makes me feel bleak.

Being a pretend grown-up woman wasn't like this. Making sketty with Dad, pushing mince round a frying pan. Carting home a set of finger-stained, second-hand cake recipe cards from a *Blue Peter* bring-and-buy sale. They came in a plastic box with a cracked lid.

'Look, Daddy, I can make rock buns, they're easy!'

And they were. Fat splodges of cake mix made with Stork SB margarine. White sugar, cheap sultanas, sometimes pink glacé cherries. Then I attempted a single-layer chocolate sponge made with cheap drinking chocolate, stirred together with a fork cos we didn't have a hand whisk. The honey-brown gloop was shoved into an old stained cake tin, and later covered in icing, which sat wonkily on the top in translucent lumpy puddles.

But most exciting of all were the real hobs and the grill on Mam's electric cooker. By the age of eight I was flicking on the switches and turning the dials right up. I'd try to get tea together, just like a real mam. Sometimes – well, many times – oil would jump out of the frying pan and burn me. Then I'd scream and I'd grizzle and Dad would appear, tutting and trying to be angry, but then he'd hug me into his belly and say, 'Why are you messing around?'

Dad knew how to make bad things feel better. He'd reach for the small canister of Burneze – a magical potion from the chemist that freezes the blister and turns the scab into a dusty, sticky war wound. Then I'd sit subdued on the sofa beside him, watching *Willo the Wisp*, sniffing back tears and looking at my battle scar, secretly proud. Two days later I would've forgotten this drama and would be making Dad cheese on toast. Like a proper mam.

'What are we having for tea, Mam?' I'd moan while watching *Hong Kong Phooey*.

She'd be trying to sew on a Brownie Badge.

'A walk round the table to see how far it is,' she'd mutter. This was her regular joke, which we never quite understood.

'No, Mam, we're really hungry, what are we having? We're starving!' Now David would join in too.

She'd sigh, looking up from her sewing.

'The kitchen is closed tonight, sorry,' she'd announce – another of her standard one-liners.

We'd groan and we'd grizzle – we knew at some point she'd stand up.

'Oh, yer as fit as I am to feed yerselves,' she'd say, but then she'd put down her needle and thread, stand up and say, 'I can do you sausage and mashed potatoes ... how does that suit you?'

Then there'd be a clanking of pots and pans and cupboard doors as she cranked into gear again, back in her place by the oven. This left her no time for her own pastimes or hobbies. Mam – like every other mam along Harold Street in Currock – never admitted she had her own dreams.

It began to occur to me as I grew bigger that being a proper grown-up woman involved being very much chained to the kitchen. At 8 a.m., at midday, at 6 p.m. too – and then there was all the shopping and the dishes to do. Life was a never-ending conveyor belt of mouths to feed – sometimes three, four or five people. Mam, feeding cold Ready Brek into stiff mouths, spooning beans onto toast, scraping watery poached eggs into bins. Cooking for all of our likes and dislikes, even when she told you straight she'd not bother.

'There's nowt worse than a fussy eater,' Mam would say. But still she managed to get something down everyone, remembering that this one didn't like peas and this one didn't like onion. She did all this without a farmers' market or reliable scales or six gas burners. She did it 365 days a year, three times a day, without anyone telling her she was clever or that it was a skill. Without ASDA deliveries, Click & Collect, Deliveroo, Uber Eats or Waitrose Rapid. She did it because mothers and wives everywhere had no choice. They did it because people get hungry continuously – it's an unavoidable truth about living. I don't want to live like this, I started to think.

Being a woman, a wife, a mammy, was less about wearing lipstick and nice frocks and more about looking like, as Mam said, 'the wreck of the *Hesperus*', in a cardigan over loose pyjama bottoms. It seemed like a lot of being knackered and fighting with a bin bag and asking for jobs to be done again and again until you finally did it yourself.

It was about putting things at the bottom of the stairs to carry up later, and being the one who says, 'OK, well, can I get you something? Are you hungry?' and then just reaching for the frying pan and making a fried-egg sandwich out of nowhere – subliminally slicing at yolks with a fish slice, then turning them over quickly, so the whole thing is done in a flash. A house needs someone at the helm, steering. And my mam steered mainly from beside the toaster, slathering slices with one hand and making a pot of tea with the other, while working out how to get our car back from the garage as the fan belt was broken. She did it while making lamb hotpot with slices of black pudding across the bottom of a scratched Pyrex dish, which she threw in the oven at four o'clock before moving the sofa to hoover, then walking me to Brownies and checking in with Gran to see if she had milk because the mobile van was fresh out again. A home needs someone elbows-deep in it, every day, constantly. Someone to do all the cleaning of bathroom floors and the de-gunking of sinks and the washing of clothes and to supervise the misery of drying socks and pants on temperamental radiators. Someone to hoover the carpets and de-flea the cat and work out what that bad smell is in the cupboard under the stairs, because it may be a rotting dead mouse. Someone to buy, write and stamp the appropriately chosen birthday cards and find a child-size

Halloween witch's outfit and get everyone ready for the wedding reception and pack suitcases for the half-term caravan holiday which Mam found in the brochure and booked.

I do not want to be a mammy, I thought.

But, I am finding that, even if there are no children, someone in every home still needs to be 'mammy'. There's still the issue of the house. If both of you are 'daddy' then kitchen surfaces stay sticky and the fridge does not refill. Cousins are in umbrage about forgotten birthday cards not posted and the petunias you bought for the window box die. Loo paper inner tubes pile up on the bathroom floor and socks smell slightly of mildew because they lingered, damp, in the machine too long.

Of course, you could share all this! Equally, respectfully and diligently. Very modern, very harmonious! But then every Saturday morning is wasted playing catch-up, trying to make light of the fact that your small window of together time now features one of you with your hand down a U-bend and the other one bleaching the wheelie bin because, well, didn't you notice there were maggots? In the beginning, Saturday mornings were for sex, eating bagels and the fresh delirium of love.

It began to occur to me in my thirties, in a dark, guilty crevice of my mind, that the only way a house works like it did in the Seventies is if one of you – regardless of gender – is 'mam'.

I shudder when I verge upon accepting this. This simply cannot be true.

When I raise it with friends they deny it, albeit weakly.

'Things have got a lot better since we got the cleaner,' they say, but they say the word cleaner quietly because they're socialists and hiring a cleaner is wrong. Actually, she's not a cleaner, really, they don't use that word, she's more a friend of the family who happens to clean.

I close the fridge door and walk back into the lounge empty-handed, where, on the television, the *MasterChef* restaurant critics – a string of very haughty, posh men with well-fed bellies and weekly columns – act outraged at the shoddy arrangement of the foie gras.

I send Just Eat a request to ask the Fortune Inn to bring my husband some Singapore noodles.

When I was a small I often read in magazines that the way to a man's heart is through his stomach. That cannot be true, I thought. It's about being lovely and pretty.

'The kitchen is closed tonight, sorry,' I say sheepishly. Within three years we were divorced.

September 2011

As I sat in bed flanked by two tabby cats googling sobering things like 'How to get a quick Decree Absolute?' or 'Am I legally married in the UK if I married in Vegas?', a lifeline arrived.

'Just wondering', said an editor at the *Evening Standard* magazine, 'if you'd like to cover our restaurant column in the back of the Friday magazine for a few weeks, just while we work out what's going on. You probably have a lot going on of an evening.'

I didn't actually have anything 'going on of an evening' right then aside from crying into a mirror and listening to Celine Dion. By day, I had a full-time role at the *Independent* newspaper writing two opinion pages per week. This was definitely distracting, but not in a terribly healthy manner.

Writing a regular weekly, or in my case bi-weekly, opinion column sends even the nicest writers slightly demented in the end. As a little girl I gobbled up pithy columns by Jean Rook, who they called 'The First Lady of Fleet Street'. That job looks marvellous, I thought. Now here I was, almost forty, in bed with a warm MacBook, surrounded by half-eaten cereal bowls, churning out thoughts. Readers, I had grown to realise, only really cared when you're furious. They liked to feel my apoplexy over pertinent topics like Arnold Schwarnenegger's lovechild or Petra Ecclestone's wedding. Twitter was not helping. Each week the Internet filleted out the more potent sections and scattergunned them across the planet.

My salary at the *Independent* was paid monthly via a Russian oligarch family called the Lebedevs. It was absurdly generous – far too generous to say no to – but then oligarchs so frequently are. The Lebedevs were raising eyebrows in London by buying up newspapers, chucking about roubles on glitzy star-filled parties, where Naomi hobnobbed with Dame Judi, as well as launching a TV channel. The Lebedevs behaved with a level of largesse and raffishness unknown to the *Guardian*. They also offered me the type of full-time employment where I didn't necessarily have to get out of bed much. It was all opinion; no interviewing, no showing my face in the Derry Street newsroom in Kensington.

'You've been lying in your bed like a coffin for nine days, princess. I think you should get up,' my friend Matt would say, in his warm, clipped Winchester College tones.

'I've been working,' I'd protest, sat in bed surrounded by half-drunk mugs of Gold Blend and Migraleve packets, having just laid down eight-hundred Pulitzer Prize-luring words on Kate Middleton's skirt length.

'Yes, I know you have been working, darling,' Matt would say. 'But how about a little shower and then meeting us in Pizza Express?'

I reread the email from the *Evening Standard* magazine, which was published every Friday and left in piles by every single London Underground station to be read by millions of commuters. In the Nineties I'd pitched features to it constantly, to no avail. Could I really cover a restaurant column? Like Michael Winner from 'Winner's Dinners'? Maybe not, but it was worth getting out of bed to try.

'Tell me a bit more,' I said on the telephone. I stalled for over eleven minutes before calling, to play it icy.

'Well, we don't have much to pay you for a fee ... but you can claim the dinner on expenses,' she said. 'We loved the funny piece you wrote for the issue Lily Allen edited. The one about hipster cafés in East London. We've had complaints!'

'About what?' I said.

'Oh, the part about cool cafés being run by lazy trust-fund brats who close for twenty-two days over Christmas and spend more time working out their slam poetry evening rota than working out a menu.'

'Oh, right, well, it's true,' I said, wincing. It sounded harsh out of context.

'We loved it, don't worry!' she said. 'OK, good,' I said.

'Can you do 625 words by next Wednesday? We'll send you some ideas of places. You're not scared of chefs, are you? We think some might get very upset.' I'm pretty sure my ability to rankle was partly why I was chosen. Restaurant critics are not there to promote chefs; they are there to sell newspapers.

'No. I'm not scared,' I said. 'I'll do it.'

But I was.

I was consumed with imposter syndrome. I knew that I definitely didn't know as much about French haute cuisine as the men with the big bellies and the tweed trousers on *MasterChef* who were furious about foie gras. But I knew enough about restaurants, surely? I'd been eating out in London for fifteen years. I knew the calendar rhythms of the food scene, how *galette de rois* in January drifts into menus full of fresh blood orange and then forced rhubarb, then asparagus and eventually all the spatchcocked horror of pheasants with their heads blasted off come the start of the shooting season on the Glorious Twelfth of August. I knew many silly things that might win me a Trivial Pursuit Food & Drink piece, like the fact that Omelette Rothschild isn't an omelette but an apricot soufflé made with Cointreau, whereas Omelette Arnold Bennett is *definitely* an omelette, made with smoked haddock, Gruyère and crème fraîche. Or that esca-beche can mean cooked but also raw. Or that *fromage de tête* may sound like posh cheese but it's actually pig's face and brain and tongue suspended horrifically in aspic.

And I loved the theatre of eating out. I loved the secret language of stupid fancy restaurants: I knew the question 'How do you want that cooked?' is actually rhetorical and you should let the chef please himself. And 'We want to make the space accessible' means we even let normals in here at lunchtime and make them vaguely welcome with a drab prix-fixe menu. And 'Can we perhaps offer you an after-dinner cocktail in the bar?' means 'Finish your pudding, we want the table back.' Surely knowing all this type of thing meant I could wing it for a few weeks in the *Evening Standard*?

So, yes, maybe I didn't know every finickity fact about Cordon Bleu cooking and there were several parts of the world I'd never visited and whose cuisine I'd never eaten, but surely that was a good thing? I could work hard and learn. I thought about the last fifteen years; all the different restau-rants, all their cliques and their sets, from the backroom at Vrisaki full of Greek Cypriot grandmas bitching about the standard of the souvlaki, to the budget pasta crowd at Pollo in Old Compton Street, to the off-duty Primrose Hill thespian wife-swapper set at The Engineer. I loved, in a twisted way, the fact that there was really no correlation at all between the actual standard of food being served and how popular a restaurant became. For years I'd eaten at MASH in London where the food bordered on inedible, but what wild pomposity it was served with! The starriness. The egos. So many actual monsters of every variety at every table across town, and worse ones behind the maître d' desk. Tired of London restaurants, tired of life, I thought.

I was quite tired of life, to be honest.

This new opportunity pretty much saved me from doing something stupid.

Soon after this conversation with the *Evening Standard* magazine, I headed off to a very hot, very upscale, no-reservations tapas joint in Fitzrovia. I took a date called Joe: another divorced fortysomething. Finding dates is easy when you're a critic; men were literally falling over themselves to let me pay for dinner. It would turn out to be one of those wretched recently divorced dates that are just an opportunity to swap horror stories about alimony settlements, while coming to the unsaid conclusion that neither of you are ready to date, before going home mutually depressed and resentful. This would all have been a lot easier to stomach if there had been food.

'Not tonight,' said the tapas bouncer. The hot, upscale tapas place demanded you turn up early to join the waiting list, so we were there by 5.30, trying to charm the aloof misery on the door.

She did not even bother to look at her clipboard – these places all seemed to have ego-typhoons on the door.

'Do you, um, y'know, want to take a phone number, in case anyone drops out?' I said.

'No one will drop out,' she said.

The no-reservations trend had recently swept into London, almost overnight, from Manhattan. Soho and Shoreditch restaurateurs loved it, as it allowed them to fill tables more efficiently, increase margins and manufacture a genre of weak buzz with little regard to how it suited customers. I already had a dim view of it, even if I knew that customers had created this situation by continuously failing to show up for tables. This led to places going bankrupt in tiny incremental stages. Still, no reservations made planning a night out with any certitude impossible. Maybe you ate, maybe you didn't. Maybe you booked a less cool back-up restaurant somewhere else and let the other poor suckers down at the last minute when you got into the buzzy place. Or maybe you didn't double-book, but instead grimly acquiesced to the fact that you and your date might spend the evening wandering forlornly around busy restaurants hoping to get seated anywhere, before retreating to a pub to drink grumpily on an empty stomach, which is what we did.

At midnight that night I opened a fresh Word document and wrote about the quiet tyranny of no reservations. I was hungry. I'd been burned by this stupid rigmarole multiple times that year – it was due a good kicking. The *Standard* may have still been working out which proper restaurant critic to give this column to, but I was not, as far as I was concerned, giving it back. Writing about restaurants felt strongly like writing about the things that were actually important in life. They would have to prise this column out of my cold, dead hands.

I looked at my heartfelt words sitting gloriously on the page and pressed 'Send'.

May 2012

'Come for dinner,' I beg Matt one Tuesday night.

'I can't,' he groans. 'Ask Tom. Ask Courtney!'

'They can't either,' I sigh.

'We won't stay late,' I plead. 'You're really good at this.'

'I can't. I need to do a presentation at 8 a.m. I can't turn up vomiting again,' he says.

Last month Matt and I went to a five-hour experimental Taiwanese tasting menu. The final course was a sugar-spun replica of a used condom on a pile of sherbet, which represented sand. The chef said the pudding was a political comment on AIDS in Asia. He had intricately piped sugar syrup into the curled-up condom to represent sperm. The restaurant charged us £520 for two people.

'I won't make you eat a condom again,' I promise.

'No. Stick me down for Saturday instead. Where is it?' he says.

'Um, it's a brasserie in a new hotel, part of a New York chain,' I say, checking my notes. 'They don't believe in plates. They serve a lot of the courses on washing lines.'

'Washing lines?' he says.

'Well, yes, the Serrano ham course definitely. They serve the lobster in a tool box.'

'OK, I'll do that one,' he says.

'I'll need to write it up on Sunday morning and brief a photographer, so it won't be a late one!' I shout as I hang up.

Everybody you meet, when you're a restaurant critic, tells you they'd love to be your dinner companion. I found this out right away when I officially accepted the role. Strangers tell you it in shops, at parties and in the street – and they really, really think they mean it. But the truth is, this comes with many caveats. What they actually mean is that they'd like to eat dinner somewhere good, preferably on a weekend and with at least some notice. These are all quite reasonable requests, but columns don't always work like that; they're always hungry for words. My friends cannot keep up with how much company I need at such short notice. The *Evening Standard Magazine* column needs to be fed at least fifty-two times a year, plus Christmas specials and end-of-year best-of lists and special commemorative themed issues. Suddenly I need to be standing up, wearing pants and out of the house a lot. Not just on weekends: on Mondays and Tuesdays and Wednesdays. And not always for lovely dinners, but some- times for wild goose chases to new openings where one sets off on the promise of a fancy Parisian-style brasserie to find it exists only in the imagination of the manager and you're actually eating stewed spaghetti in a stairwell. Or the chef has had a breakdown at the fancy concept restaurant and closed without any warning. Or, the worst of all situations, it's a tiny independently owned place that is not interesting enough to write about and far too fragile to criticise in print, so halfway through the main course, I'm making a reservation some-where else.

'Grace and Flavour' – the rather ingenious title that *ES Magazine* conjured up for my column, which I love – is gain-ing momentum. I've begun to hone my restaurant critic voice and work out my audience. 'Grace and Flavour' is for Londoners who are interested in eating out but don't feel remotely like part of the food scene in-crowd. They might be too scared to call up or go to a fancy place, like I was with Moro. I'm writing it for them: I go in first to do a recce. I'm writing for people like Courtney, my friend who has two babies and, in the middle of the night, sometimes feels like she'll never get dressed up and go out again. I'm writing for anyone who's saved up all month for dinner and does not want to end up in a stairwell eating pasta bow-ties in ketchup, or a political sugar condom with syrup jizz and sherbet sand. I'm writing for people who cannot afford any of these silly places but want to read something that makes them laugh while standing with their face in a stranger's armpit on the Northern Line. And I'm hoping to attract a regular audience of those who don't quibble at flowery prose about the clien-tele, the hand-soap and my love life on the occasions when I've blatantly run out of steam about the rigatoni. Thankfully, there must be thousands of people like this out there because, within about a year, I'm one of the most read online columns at the newspaper.

'Well, we had our teas at Hungry Horse,' says Mam when I phone her. 'Yer' dad had gammon with a grilled pineapple ring. It was quite adventurous for him.'

'What is a Hungry Horse?' I say.

'It's a family pub. They do mixed grills. When are you going to write about that?'

'I'm thinking probably never,' I laugh.

'Are people still liking your food column?' she asks. She's definitely pleased I'm leaving the house more.

'Well,' I hesitate, 'the readership grows every week. They tell me the online figures. I'm probably their most read columnist right now, so I think so'

Actually, several people are really quite furious – chefs, chef's wives, other restaurant critics, investors, public relations teams, strangers on Twitter, and so on. Some tell me I have no business writing about food; I'm no match for the greats, like A.A. Gill, Charles Campion, Matthew Fort or Michael Winner. Why am I being taken seriously? Surely, I'm only there due to a fluke?

But, I think, my life has been a fluke since I was a little girl watching the Motherwell train whip past on its way to Euston, as I ate pickled eggs by the track.

What do people imagine I will do if they don't approve of me? Take the hint and stop?

March 2013

'He was in your room, unpacking your bras? I don't think I'd like it,' says Mam.

I'm telling her about a stay at the Connaught hotel the night before where the suite came with its own personal butler. I was writing for the *Evening Standard* about one of the fanciest ways to spend a Staycation in the capital and how it feels to have a butler running your bath, choosing your bath oils, arranging your tights and shoes into charming piles. This suite made the place I stayed in Vienna back in the Nineties feel like the Novotel in Ipswich town centre. However, I really wasn't terribly good at having a butler. After rejecting all of Kaspar's kind offers to help me arrange holistic beauty treatments and private viewings at art galleries, I opted for a quiet dinner in the room. This placated him a little; he appeared at 7 p.m. on the dot, pushing a trolley with a silver cloche on it, which he then transferred to the grand oval table, where he arranged Sole Meunière, pommes mousseline and a side of cavolo nero into a fabulous dinner for one. This world would be lovely, I found myself thinking, if I had someone special to share it with; even if I did give my divorce lawyers permission to shoot me with a harpoon gun if I ever again mentioned getting wed.

'I wish you could have been there,' I say to Mam. 'If you come down, we could come here for afternoon tea.'

Mam takes some convincing to come to London these days. She says all the walking around tires her out, not like when we came sightseeing when I was small. She'd walk us from Big Ben to Hamleys and back via Buckingham Palace without a thought. Now she's not as mobile. I also know that taking Dad anywhere far from his front door these days is a battle, as he complains too much.

'Well, me, Dad, Dave, Tam and Lola went to the Wetherspoon's in Keswick,' she says. 'Five of us had dinner. The bill with drinks was thirty-two quid! I had the buttermilk chicken burger.'

'It sounds delicious,' I say, deadpan.

'Oh, you're a snob, you are,' she laughs.

The truth is that when I squeeze in time to come to Cumbria, taking Dad to the local Wetherspoon's near my brother's house in Keswick is one of the unlikely high points. I always have the same specific items on the menu: the Mexican veggie burger with onion rings, plus an enormous glass of Echo Falls Chardonnay. If you buy two, they give you the bottle. This doesn't happen in the Connaught Bar. And Wetherspoon's is the only time Dad really relaxes. If we get him a bottle of Doom Bar, the clouds in his brain seem to dissipate for a little while. He forgets whatever thing is currently making him anxious, like the Carlisle Council recycling schedule, which he is currently fixated on. Which item goes in which box? What day will it go? How about on a bank holiday? It's also a pleasure to see him eating. Dad has been losing weight recently. He will rarely agree to a full plate of food. Everything offered to him needs to be taken back to the kitchen in their flat in Carlisle and halved. Mam says that, on the upside, his sugar intake is more under control. The hospital says his blood tests are much improved – but if his blood is better, that doesn't explain his odd behaviour.

'I actually don't mind Wetherspoon's,' I tell Mam on the phone. 'It's that Brewers Fayre with the ball pond where I draw the line.'

'Oh, Lola loved that ball pond as a toddler,' Mam laughs. 'And the chicken poppers.'

'Yes, but I have a very refined palate,' I say starrily to make her laugh.

The truth is my palate has altered a bit. I can now tell the difference by sniffing between champagne, Cava Brut, a Chablis Premier Cru and a Pouilly-Fuissé.

Or tell a beurre noir from a beurre blanc or a beurre noisette. I'm by no means infallible: I messed up in a column recently, confusing black cod and blackened cod – black cod being a specific type of cod (the blackness does *not* refer to the miso glaze), while blackened cod is cod with cayenne pepper seasoning. But after a week of online unpleasantness and questions about why my job isn't taken off me, I'll not make that error again. A few nights before the Connaught I'd reviewed a place in Chelsea where I was handed a tasting menu, mainly in French, filled with the obscure glands and valves of animals, rare fruits that are only in season for three weeks and micro herbs grown specially in polytunnels only for that kitchen. I sat at the chef's table with the sort of elegant people who refuse the chives and vinaigrette with oysters, preferring to sip the sea water straight from the shell and then claim to know the difference between the minerals in the North Sea and the Atlantic Ocean. One course involved large chunks of bone marrow in raw egg.

'Was your dinner nice?' says Mam. She is so proud of me.

'To be honest, not really, no,' I say.

CHAPTER 9

Monsters

October 2013

When the offer arrives via email, I examine it carefully to check it isn't Matt playing a prank. It looks bona fide, but it seems almost ludicrous. Terrifying and ludicrous – but also too amazing to refuse.

Four weeks later, a Mercedes-Benz picks me up from my house to take me to the set of BBC One's *MasterChef: The Professionals*, where I've been invited to be one of the critics. In the car, I feel so absolutely bilious with nerves I doubt I can swallow. Let alone swallow with TV cameras in my face and then discuss the intricate juxtaposition of jus and gel in erudite terms with Jay Rayner and William Sitwell either side. My thoughts turn to Dad. *MasterChef* has been on TV for thirty years, ever since a rather funny man with a sing-song voice called Loyd Grossman presented it. Loyd would invite serious French chefs to *deliberate, cogitate and digest* haute cuisine cooked by earnest amateurs. Me and Dad would laugh when Loyd called a custard slice by its posh name, millefeuille, pronounced *'mieeeefieeeeeu'*, sounding like a drunken dairy cow. Or when we learned that hen-of-the-woods is actually a fancy mushroom, not a big hen, or that *tarte Tatin aux pommes* is pronounced *ta-ta-tah-oh-pom* and is just apple pie.

'Look at these silly sods,' Dad would say as he sat in his chair eating an ASDA choc-ice. 'Look at this one in the tweed. He looks like Rupert Bear!'

The car arrives on set, a TV producer in a headset rushes towards the outdoor smoking area and chivvies the contestants along, herding them away from my sight. Secrecy is paramount. The less information I have about who is cooking today, the better. The fewer things we know, the more natural our reactions will be when the chefs bowl through the doors carrying seared duck breast with enoki and pickled mooli.

'Grace Dent is on set, door three, walking now,' says the producer as I step out of the car.

'This way,' she says, leading me through a maze of kitchens, past shelves of pans and plates and cutlery, past racks of chef's whites and buckets of dirty dishes. Gregg Wallace shoves his head around part of the set as I walk, takes one look at me and shouts, 'Oh, it's you! I like you! Welcome to *MasterChef*, Miss Dent!'

I'm left in a dressing room with a full-length mirror, a bowl of grapes and a large framed picture of John Torode. I breathe in and breathe out.

I've decided to wear my hair down rather than in a beehive so that I don't look too severe and antagonise the audience

– or more accurately Twitter, which I can't really look at anymore as the strangers' comments are too upsetting. Later, at the critics' table, as each dish arrives, I find myself being resolutely positive about each element. I cut all the chefs some slack. After all, they're probably nervous too, like me. They could be having an off day. That's why their emulsion split and their béchemel tastes of flour. That's why their rainbow chard is gritty and their chocolate crémeaux is a brown puddle. I don't want to look like a ball breaker in the edit – I can't face the blowback online. Jay Rayner from the *Observer* and William Sitwell, editor of *Waitrose Magazine*, are much more certain in their views. They're much more offended by the droopy soufflé and the overdone halibut. Not just offended. Slightly outraged. They know how to deliver great telly. Worse still, when the second chef unveiled his rather delicious plate of monkfish, I suddenly found my appetite and gobbled down the lot.

'You need to pace yourself, darling,' says Jay. 'There are five more plates to go.'

'Oh I'm fine, I'm starving,' I say. But by the time the last chef arrives, clutching calves liver in a port reduction, my face is a tad green.

I escape from the day's filming without humiliating myself, at least, but I feel a little like I've let myself down. In the final edit, I get eight seconds maximum on camera, meekly head tilting like Princess Diana, saying the duck and the soufflé were lovely but the fish, not very controversially, 'isn't very nice'.

Matt, Tom and Courtney find my demure pose hilarious, and circulate the clip via email, playing it again and again. They laugh and laugh.

'I think you need to be more you,' says Tom.

'Just tell them the truth,' says Courtney.

Next time I vow to build my hair up big and walk with my shoulders back, like I'm completely meant to be there, to deliver some home truths. There's no place on primetime telly for polite ambivalence.

Over the following year, being an increasingly familiar face on *MasterChef* begins to change everything. From that moment on, I gave up my right to eat dinner in private anywhere ever again.

When you appear on *MasterChef*, everyone from school mams buying Weetabix in the B&M Store to yuppies in the Farrow & Ball shop to flight attendants to traffic wardens to bin men to the woman who's doing your smear test will stop, squint, and say, 'Oh, hang on, I know you!'

The show, after thirty years and hundreds of hopeful contestants, is still so well loved by people from every demographic; it's watched by folk of all ages, faiths, races and of every class. Just as me and my dad loved watching fancy food people getting overexcited about scallops, now people watch me with their own kids. It's just a simple show where people cook and others judge, but it's captured the nation's heart. Deep down we are all food critics.

April 1976

We're on holiday at Pontins near Southport.

Me, Dad, Mam, Dave and Bob.

There's a fancy-dress competition and I'm a bunny rabbit. I put my blue gymnastic leotard on over white woolly tights. My bunny ears are Dad's Odor-Eaters. The winner is a ghost, draped in bed sheets.

Afterwards there is a 'Dance with your Dad' contest. We spin around the floor to 'Silver Lady' by David Soul, then Baccara's 'Yes Sir, I Can Boogie'.

My tiny feet fit on top of his big feet.

Whenever we walk around the holiday camp people tell Mam that my little brother David is gorgeous. They say nothing about me, as I'm not. I know I'm strange-looking – my eyes a touch squinty, my teeth wonky.

Dad says I am lovely, though. I am his only little girl. I eat mashed potato and battered fish in the Pontins canteen each teatime. Mam toasts crumpets with jam in our chalet before bed. I am fast asleep by seven, after half an hour of insisting I'm not going to bed.

At night I wake from nightmares and appear beside Mam and Dad's bed, crying.

'Can I gerrin?' I say, crawling in between them where I carve out a space to lie in. Sweaty, wriggly.

I sleep with a foot in Mam's back and a hand in Dad's bristly face.

In the morning Dad wakes up grumbling.

'How is she here?' he says. 'Does she not have her own bed?'

'She was scared,' Mam mumbles. 'Of monsters.'

Dad pokes me in the stomach. He knows I am listening.

'So if the monsters come from here and there,' he says, pointing to both sides of the bed, 'you'll be here in the middle, safe.'

'Yes,' I say, opening my eyes, giggling.

'Monsters?' he says.

'Yes,' I say. 'Monsters.'

Carlisle, August 2016

'Grace, are you there? Are you there, Grace?'

'Yes, I'm here, Dad. Are you OK?'

It's 3 a.m.

'Yeah, I'm OK, presh,' he begins. 'I'm just thinking. I need to get a ladder.'

'Why?' I say, sitting up.

There is a long silence. I am lying in bed in their flat in Carlisle. For months Mam's health has been trickling downhill. She assures me it's nothing – first a cold that won't leave, or perhaps a chest infection, then almost certainly, an interim doctor assures me, bronchitis.

It's certainly not cancer, nothing to worry about, and don't worry about Dad, Dad is fine too, don't worry about us.

For the last year the saga of Mam's breathing has been flickering in the background of phone calls home. I've tried to keep an eye on it from afar; I liaise with Dave and Tam each day and grab days in the North when I can, but it's not working. Not properly. Not like it would if I was there all the time. It's too easy to lose track of doctor's appointments and what has been prescribed and if it's worked and what is being hidden. Mam has been playing down her illness to everyone close. Her doctor sent her away multiple times with instructions to rest and drink Benylin, before eventually giving her antibiotics, then more antibiotics, until eventually, after three months, she couldn't walk or even stand up and was rushed to hospital. Dave called me as I was about to go on stage to talk at the Edinburgh Festival.

I descended on Carlisle, all sharp elbows with a notepad and pen, looking for answers and promises. Mam was in a ward for people with heart problems. The nurses looking after her there had no clue as to why she was breathless but were at least kind and made me tea.

Mam was fading. She was washed out and lifeless. All the colour in her cheeks had gone. And there I was, the pushy daughter from London, the one who wanted to solve problems by asking the right people the right questions. The one who wanted to speed things up and get her the right course of treatment. The one who wanted to know why we were in the heart unit when this seemed to have nothing to do with her heart.

No one was able to help me.

But of course there was tea if I wanted it.

A specialist may be around later, they told me, but it's Thursday heading into a bank holiday weekend, so you probably won't see him until Tuesday.

Mam's biggest concern was my dad. He couldn't be left alone.

'I've told the nurses he has dementia,' she said. 'They've put him in the office until someone could come.' It was the first time the word had come out of her mouth.

I nodded, because I knew it too.

Dad taps again at the bedroom door.

'What's up, Dad?' I say, trying to sound very calm. 'I need to get up into the attic,' Dad says, poking his nose around the door.

Dad's enormous nose.

'It's a Roman nose,' he used to say to me. 'It's a Roman all over my face!'

Dad appears in the room. In a white vest and pyjama bottoms, much more unshaven than he would usually allow himself to be.

'I need to get up there,' he says. He points at the ceiling. 'And, y'know, get behind the box and, well … y'know … do you know?'

'OK,' I say, doing the calm voice that I find works. 'Well, let's not go up there now. It will be dark up there now. Why don't we do it first thing in the morning? It's 3 a.m. now. Let's get in the attic and find it when it's light.'

He thinks a little, then he nods.

'OK, presh, yeah, OK, when it's light. We'll do it then. The attic will be dark, won't it?'

He goes back to bed. This is a flat. They do not have an attic.

I lie in bed and have a small, thoroughly futile cry. Dad gets back into his bed, but he does not switch his bedside lamp off as he is lying there waiting for the daylight so we can begin our job.

Carlisle, October 2016

Me, Mam and Dad are eating toast in their flat in Carlisle and watching *Homes Under the Hammer*.

Mam is eighty but adamant that cancer, in all the various places it has appeared, will not stop her, even if the pills and injections make her sick and tired.

'Well, I've had a good innings,' she says. Or, 'Well, it is what it is, it's just a pain in the arse.' Dad's dementia has no diagnosis. Mam says he doesn't need one yet as she can carry on looking after him. I'm on one of my two-day quickfire visits to Carlisle. I know it's not enough. David lives in Keswick, 35 miles away from Carlisle; I live 260 miles away in London. It would work so much better if we were all under the same roof. We could concentrate on getting Dad a proper diagnosis and caring for Mam properly.

I travel on the Virgin West Coast train, back and forth, forth and back, living in a spin between London and Carlisle, tearing through four or five restaurants a week to keep the column afloat, but the food is hard to stomach. My house in London becomes unloved and then unlovable. The pyracantha overgrows into a wall of dead black spikes, the lawn dies, Japanese knotweed takes root under the path and begins to kill one of the trees. Rats move into the ceiling in the kitchen and eat all the wiring in the kitchen spotlights. Geno, one of my beloved cats – the nearest thing I have to children – tires of being chucked biscuits by a cat sitter and moves in with the neighbours without a backwards glance. When I attempt to reclaim him, he lies impassively on their sofa, feigning amnesia.

'When you were a kitten, I slept on my back for six months, so you could sleep in my armpit!' I fumed.

In Carlisle, Dad stands by my bed at 3 a.m. in his flat cap and jacket, asking when we're going out to ASDA. He will not grasp in any meaningful sense that Mam is ill. He has the news broken to him afresh each day. His reaction ranges from crying to petulant anger to saying we are trying to trick him.

I attempt to explain that Mam needs rest, that the treatment she's having to contain the spread in her bones is brutal, that she is now the patient. But he walks about almost all of the night, so she can't sleep and I can't sleep and Dave can't sleep. We are all sleepless.

If I can get a diagnosis, maybe we can get proper help.

But I'm scared that if I let other people in on our secret, we may have to let him go to a home.

There is so much I want to say to Dad, but I can't bring myself to.

Dementia is really awkward.

Not just painful and frightening. Embarrassing.

I don't like to be left alone with Dad. If I'm never left alone with Dad, it won't be my responsibility to say, 'Look, Dad, do you think you have dementia?'

Which is the start of a chat that means: 'So, Dad, shall we talk about the fact that you've been handed a hideous, terrifying extended death sentence, which is making you humiliate yourself in public and will make our family splitting up and strangers looking after you inevitable?

But sometimes I can see terror in his eyes.

Sometimes, as Dad talks nowadays, midway through a nonsensical sentence his brain catches up. And right then he understands the total ridiculousness of what he is saying, and then pure shame passes across his face. I noted this last Christmas.

I find that shame so cutting. It hurts my heart. It stays with me all the time when I am back in London. I cannot eat the dinners I am supposed to review.

Sometimes, as my dad talks nowadays, midway through a nonsensical sentence he stops for a moment like his brain is catching up … but then he just carries on, becoming more nonsensical until he trails off, having completely lost the thread of his original idea.

Which one is worse? When he is conscious of his brain decaying and therefore panicked, or when he is blissfully unaware, completely barmy and also quite frightening to be with?

Sometimes I get up the nerve to ask him a question in soft words and cushioned terms. 'Are you feeling like you forget stuff, Dad? Like when you got up for work the other morning … did you forget you've retired?' But then he will deny it or pretend not to hear. Or he just tells me plainly no. I wonder if I should track down his other children, wherever they are, and warn them it's now or never. They would need to come now if they want to catch a tiny glimpse of the man he was. But that feels like I'm asking for help during the worst times. He wasn't there for them during the good days. Also, Dad's in no state to be ambushed by an awkward family reunion. I put that dilemma from my mind. This is our problem – mine and David's – the two kids he didn't walk out on. We can cope.

At least, I thought we could. But too many bad things are happening at once now. We are struggling. Something has to give.

CHAPTER 10

Your Own Personal Toby

October 2016

It's more difficult to walk through Euston without being recognised since I told one of the *Celebrity MasterChef* contestants that I wouldn't feed his turd-like churros to a Labrador. Or another one who came along clutching gazpacho that there was no place in civilised society for his cold soup. But even if my face is a little more recognisable or I've got my own Radio 4 show, these things feel a touch hollow. Nothing really matters aside from Mam and Dad. When your heart is in shreds, being pointed at by strangers in Tesco Express isn't much of a sticky plaster.

On the train I look again through the rental deeds. It's a large bungalow with many bedrooms, plenty of space and – most important of all – a big dining room with a huge table. It's close to my brother's work in the Lake District. It's a crackpot plan and it might bankrupt me, but it feels right. If we can all eat together every night, we can be like a proper family. We can have one final crack at normal again before it's taken away. Is this insane? Am I doing the right thing? Can I possibly move back to Cumbria? I've cased out all the ways to make life in the Lakes easier. ASDA will deliver food to the bungalow – the nearest one is thirty-five miles away. Amazon Prime will deliver almost anything else I need and leave it in a locker at an Esso garage one mile from the house within around forty-eight hours. There's a small, rural Co-op with fresh vegetables within two miles; except I can't drive. In fact I've failed my test so many times it deserves its own certificate from the DVLA. I remind myself that my gran and her sisters managed to stay fed and alive in rural Cumberland in the 1920s by sharing one push-bike and killing their own pig. I can make this work. On the train up north, I make a deal with myself that this isn't going home forever. This isn't the end of the road. I still own a house in London, even if it is full of cobwebs and dead plants. I'm still a Londoner. I'll use this time, in a bungalow on a hill caring for a woman with cancer and a man with dementia, to grow spiritually, read all the Booker Prize winners and work on my conversational Mandarin. I don't have to start wearing GORE-TEX leggings and tying my hair in a top knot all day. I don't have to start drinking at 4 p.m., like I have been during my mercy missions to Cumbria – by pouring a large glass of Aldi Merlot and having a shuffle through *Pick Me Up* magazine – even if it feels nice. I can still do my job, can't I? I just need to be more organised. I can whistlestop home once a month to London, eat four times in different restaurants, grab my post and come back. Also, I need to use my train hours wisely. If anything, this is the year I will finally begin writing the HBO-purchased screenplay that wins me an Emmy. I won't stay in the North forever. Unless I meet a multi-millionaire septuagenarian landowner with a bad heart who needs a wife. No, not even then.

Dave picks me up at Penrith station.

'You look knackered, moon face,' he says.

'I am,' I say. 'How is Dad coping with the bungalow?'

'He's roaming around the corridors asking Mam when they're going home ten times an hour,' says Dave wearily.

We play Public Enemy all the way back to our new home.

'Hey, Dad,' I say, wheeling in two suitcases and an enormous rucksack.

'Home?' he says.

'This is me now. I'm going to stay here for a while full time. I've come back.'

Dad begins to speak. In his head it is school home time and I've moved his newspaper, which is his only pleasure in life. It is 1970, he's late for Sergeant's Mess dinner and he's lost his right cufflink. Where is yer mam? he asks. Where is yer mam? This is all in the same sentence. All the moments of his life squeezed together to form a note, then expanding back out together. Having emitted the noise, he closes his eyes.

'It's not really the big homecoming I imagined,' I say to Dave, as Dad begins to snore.

We both laugh.

'Do you want a beer?' he says, handing me a tin.

Carlisle, March 2017

'Well, that's a turn up for the books,' I say to Dad. He nods at me, but I'm not sure he understands. The nurse at the blood clinic says Dad no longer seems to have diabetes. He weighs six stone eleven – he looks like a little sparrow – but now that he is no longer interested in food, his blood is now in much better shape. Despite the decades of doughnuts and Dairy Milk, Dad hasn't lost either of his feet. Now he hardly eats at all. This is the tiniest of victories.

It's 9 a.m. at the infirmary and I'm wearing an oversized man's North Face fleece jacket over GORE-TEX leggings. All my Shellac nails have fallen off and I am becoming lackadaisical about moustache bleaching. It's safe to say the standards on Brand Grace Dent have fallen. Today's breakfast was a piece of millionaire's shortbread from the charity tuck shop, served to me by one of the Gnome brigade from my old Brownie Pack, who had salt 'n' pepper hair and the sort of eye bags that suggested she'd adhered obediently for decades to our Brownie mantra of helping everyone before herself. I have yet to begin writing an Emmy-award-winning rom-com, but I do have some hot tips on how to cajole a man with dementia into drinking a Complan calorie-fortified milk drink while he is shouting 'fuck off!'

Dad's behaviour is becoming quite frightening. He makes wild, paranoid accusations that we've stolen his belongings. We have killed his cat. We are all in a conspiracy against him.

Sometimes he is blunt and really quite cutting, bringing up my appearance, my lack of children, my failed marriage. He says that there's something wrong with my head. I feign deafness or simply laugh, but later hide in my bedroom and cry angrily. How bloody dare he? I think. He had five kids. Me and Dave are the only ones still here. What if I leave too? The following morning Dad is soft and sweet once more. I'm reminded that I love him again.

After several more months in a haze of guilt and sadness, David and I sneak out for thirty minutes alone in a local pub. We're exhausted. For a fortnight we've watched Mam struggle on, recovering from her latest chemo injections, which we hope will halt the spread in her brain and bone. Mam needs sleep and silence, but Dad's is up all night, shouting and pacing. We make a pact to find someone who'll listen to us about Dad. A social worker, a doctor, someone. Every option we think of seems frightening. But we have to do it. Even if this means letting outsiders come into the bungalow, snooping about and judging us for our failings. Even if we have to try and sort out legal power of attorney over Dad's medical choices, which we've read will cost £700 pounds in solicitor's fees. We have to do these things, even if we both know that by doing them we are setting the ball rolling to splitting us up as a family. We go back and forth endlessly between the pros and cons of keeping us all together or giving Mam a fighting chance of survival by splitting us up. Both choices are terrible. I cry into a warm, stale glass of pub Pinot Grigio and David necks his pint. He sticks his enormous arm around me and says, 'It'll be right, we can sort this out.' His face looks unsure.

We make numerous phone calls and leave messages on answer machines, and eventually a social worker arrives at the bungalow. Her policy seems to be not to talk to us. Dad must explain for himself what's happening over an informal cup of tea. But the only reliable faculty Dad has left is being able to hide his madness when strangers appear. He softens his face and smiles and answers all her questions very vaguely.

The lady goes away quite happily, telling us she'll write a report.

Each time we make a small step towards getting a diagnosis, we have a setback and then, as a family, we lose heart in pushing for the truth.

'I think she's right. I think he is more or less fine,' says Mam.

'Sometimes I don't think it is as bad as he is making out,' says Dave.

And then we are back to square one.

April 2017

I'm roasting a chicken for tea and Dad is helping, because nothing goes on in this house that he doesn't have his nose in. Any rustling of supermarket carrier bags, any raised voices, any arrival through the door in our bungalow in Keswick.

We walk around the tiny Co-op sometimes, me and him, down the aisle together. I never let the trolley, with his small hands attached, out of my sight.

I might only need bits. Dave waits outside for us. We just go there to get out of the house.

'Whoopsies!' he'll say, pointing at a cheap apple pie, reduced from a pound to twelve pence.

'Whoopsies!' I'll laugh and stick it in our trolley.

As lots of the things I loved about my family dissolved or grew frightening, a trip to the supermarket became one of the only things we had left.

I steam some broccoli and add plenty of butter. I shake parboiled potatoes in flour then oil and chuck them in a very hot oven. All Dad's really bothered about is pudding. Or, better still, a bar of chocolate at the end. I will never see Cadbury's chocolate without thinking of my father. Cadbury's purple is love. Cadbury's purple is us toddling slowly back from the NAAFI shop before he left the forces. And now, in 2017, Cadbury's is one of the only things I can ever guarantee he will eat.

As I pierce the chicken's skin to see if the juice is clear, Dad hangs about by the hob. His blue, inky tattoo sags on his lower right arm because his flesh doesn't fit his body anymore.

I never did get him to answer questions about it. Now I never will. Meanwhile, his questioning of me is constant. The same questions over and over again.

Do I know where his razor is?

Has Mam told me where she put his razors?

It is one of his recurring themes.

'Mind what yer doin'. Yer don't wannalerritburn,' he says as I scrape the pan and make gravy.

'I'm not lerrin' it burn,' I say, my accent still riven with his Merseyside tones. Eventually he loses interest and walks off. The Wi-Fi in the bungalow is so unreliable that I have taken to listening to BBC Radio Cumbria on Dad's wireless, which plays a heady mix of Perry Como classics and memories of the Dalemain Marmalade Festival. I wonder what is happening in London. Rush hour, fancy launches, restaurants opening their doors for the evening's service. I'd rather be here; carving the chicken, mashing potatoes, laying roasties in a large bowl beside the buttered broccoli and carrots. I lay everything out on the side in pans so my family can assemble in an orderly queue and serve themselves. Dad can no longer go to Toby's, as he would find it too frightening. So now I make it come to him.

'Tea is rrrrrready!' I shout like a foghorn. I've given up calling it dinner.

Mam appears looking pale. Her long blonde hair is now very short and silver. Her pills make her stable but suppress her pleasure in eating. Feeding her meals that she can enjoy is one of my greatest joys. I even love it when she revolts at my attempt to feed her more ambitious things, like couscous, which 'tastes like the bottom of a parrot cage'. Or tofu, which is 'deep fried sanitary pad'. Mam's fighting spirit is in there somewhere. The pilot light is still flickering. I'm on much safer ground if I make a roast dinner.

'Ooh lovely,' she says. 'Chicken.'

'Get in the queue, you,' I say. 'Typical bloody pensioner.'

She laughs and pinches a small, crispy roast potato.

Dad appears and tells me he is not hungry, but I hand him a plate anyway and let him come to the front of the queue.

iPhone note: Things Dad will eat if I am not there.

White toast with butter and cheap marmalade.

He likes a soft, fresh brown roll with a bit of something on it. You need to underplay it when you describe it. Do not call it a cheese roll. Or a ham roll. Call it a small roll with a little bit of cheese.

Toast with strong spready cheese.

Three fish fingers, a little bit of tartare sauce, no bread.

Smoked mackerel flaked on toast with a blob of mayo.

A mild chicken curry ready-meal with rice (don't bother with naan bread or anything).

Two sausages with a fried egg (or don't bother with the egg) and ketchup.

Sliced corned beef on a roll with a bit of ketchup.

Chunky veg soup that comes in a plastic carton. Serve him half. No bread.

Tins of Scotch broth soup. He will send back all the bits.

Breaded cod and about eight oven chips. Salt, vinegar, tartare sauce.

A boiled egg (no bread).

Choc-ice, like a Magnum Mini.

Glass of Merlot with dinner. He will find any bottle of port.

October 2017

'Can I pencil you in for twenty-second of November for *MasterChef*? It's you, Jay Rayner and Tom Parker Bowles. Can you be in London for then? Congratulations on the new job by the way! This is huge!' says Vanessa, my TV agent. I am outside the front door of the bungalow, looking across at Latrigg Fell, trying to let Mam sleep. She is zapped on injections and strong pills. Dad is asleep too. Or at least I thought he was.

Inside the hallway I can hear a clattering. A drawer opening and closing.

'Thank you,' I say quietly, as I've not told anyone up north yet. Saying yes to it was ludicrous. 'Hang on, Vanessa – Dad, what do you need?'

I've found Dad's wandering stage the hardest.

First you hear a rustle. Then the familiar sounds of someone searching for something. Kitchen cupboards open, then close again. Drawers creak open, back and forth, and then the footsteps head back to the bedroom and back to the corridor, wandering between the lounge and the kitchen.

Rooting through the phone table's drawer. Things being overturned again and again in the drawer. And then silence. And then five minutes later the whole routine happens again from the start.

'What have you lost, Dad?' I say. Dad is examining pens, some old receipts, an old phone cable, and putting them back in the drawer again.

252

Sometimes Dad is very annoyed about this missing item. Sometimes he's quiet. But it's always the same item. His razor.

'Mam brought me a razor home from shopping,' he says. 'Have you seen it?'

'OK,' I say. 'Do you think it's in the drawer?'

His expression looks wary, like I am trying to trick him.

'I – well, I dunno,' he says. 'I'm lookin' for it.'

We have bought Dad two different electric razors. We find them broken up into pieces; the cogs, the batteries, the innards all taken out and unravelled.

As my father's translator-in-chief, my guess is he can feel the hair growing on his face, which makes him want to shave. However, when he is faced with the mirror he doesn't recognise himself or grasp what needs to be done. If me or Dave try to shave him ourselves, he becomes angry. If Dave takes him to the barber, we have to pretend that it is perfectly normal to be taken there like a child, but we have no idea how he will react, once he's there.

And then the hair grows back in a couple of days anyhow, and the pattern begins again. Searching.

'Dad,' I say, 'give me a minute. I'll look for it. Sit down, I'll make you a cup of tea.'

Sometimes distraction with tea or cake works.

Up and down the corridor he walks, up and down, looking. Overturning boots in the shoe rack and looking behind coats and opening and closing that same drawer.

'Dave bought me a new razor yesterday,' he says again.

Sometimes he sounds so convincing.

And this is possible.

We are all so tired and no longer relaying information to each other. We are all becoming mad. Mam hasn't slept properly for weeks. Dad will not let her out of his sight. If I separate him from her, he asks again and again where Mam has gone. When he wakes in the night to wander around, he wants Mam to be awake too.

Then, one morning, in the midst of the madness, a job offer. The *Guardian* newspaper wonder if I'd consider the role of restaurant critic; not merely reviewing in London, but right across the British Isles. Fifty-two columns per year, plus Christmas holiday specials. I can write about Scotland, Wales, Cornwall, Northern Ireland, wherever I want, sometimes even in Europe. The online site is read widely in America and Australia. I read the email quietly at 5 a.m. while drinking Gold Blend on the bungalow step. Even considering this offer feels selfish. I'd need to be away more. But these jobs come up very rarely. How can I possibly say no?'

November 2017

Despite Dad falling out of bed quite badly, hurting his head and back, he seems to be having quite a good day out at the Cumberland Infirmary with his kids. He's chirpier now than when we went to Alton Towers in the Eighties. He's telling jokes, reciting poetry we've never heard before and is in great spirits. My patience, on the other hand, is threadbare. The staff have lost Dad's admission form. I do not recognise myself sometimes these days. I am always angry. The fury bubbles behind my eyes permanently, but I can't pinpoint why. I'm furious about the bleak existential reality that everything we love and hold dear must grow old, fragile and die at some time, which I've sort of always known but have ignored all my life, but here it is in living colour – or rather, here it is in the greys and browns and sludge-like shades of NHS buildings and in the stench of disinfectant and in the chaos of lost admission notes.

'Hello, Mr Dent, how are you?' says a nurse, sweeping the curtains aside as she goes.

Dad says something surreal. Skirting board? Orange? Army?

'Dad has dementia,' I say to the new nurse. I've told the last three nurses.

She nods at me as if she is listening, but she is not. It is not on his medical record as we have no diagnosis and the nurse is so busy herself she doesn't have time to decipher whether I'm telling the truth.

'So, Mr Dent, are you taking any medication right now? Do you know off-hand the names of what you are taking?' she says. 'Are you registered with a GP in Carlisle?'

'Dad has dementia,' I say. 'Can you ask me these questions? I can tell you the answers.'

She ignores me.

'Do you know your date of birth?' she says. '1973,' he says

'No, you're older than that.'

The nurse laughs.

But I'm not laughing.

Me and Dave sit for hours after this in the corridor of the Cumberland Infirmary, in a cramped walkway with a queue of elderly people lying on trolleys. The vending machines are all empty, so I can't even get Dad some Dairy Milk. The automatic door is broken. It feels like a terrible humanitarian disaster has happened, but it hasn't; this is just an average Saturday in a regional NHS hospital.

We are finally called in to see yet another nurse. 'Hello, Mr Dent,' she says. 'Now, what happened to you today? Are you on any medication right now? I need to check some details. Now, who is your doctor?'

'Hello, I'm his daughter. My father has dementia. Can you ask me these questions? It will be faster.'

'Has he?' says the woman.

'Yes,' I say.

'OK, Mr Dent, what is your date of birth?' she says, carrying on regardless. 'Where is your admission form? Did you bring any paperwork with you?'

'That paperwork went missing,' I say.

'OK, why don't we start that form again from the beginning? George, are you registered with a GP in Carlisle? What is your postcode?'

'Liverpool, I'm a Scouser,' says my father.

'You live in Liverpool?'

'My father has dementia,' I say again. I need to get Dad a diagnosis.

'OK, we're just going to pop you back in the corridor for a while, then maybe we should start that admission form again. I think it was probably left on the side by the ambulance when you were having the X-ray. Are you the daughter?' the nurse says.

'Yes, I'm the daughter,' I say.

'This is my little girl,' says Dad, smiling. I reach out and hold his hand.

Carlisle, 1981

The vestibule door opens. I can hear the television in the living room playing *Nationwide* with Frank Bough louder now. My father is standing there with a plate. He lets out a laugh when he sees me.

'Worryadoin' in here, princess?' he says.

'I wanna sleep here,' I say.

'Yer Mam said. You wanna live in the vestibule?'

'Yeah, just for tonight. I wanna sleep here.'

'You've got a screw loose, you have,' he says.

'No, I've not,' I say. But even at this early age I know I have a bit.

'Mam says you've gotta eat some of your tea,' he says. He passes me the plate with cheese-and-ham Findus Crispy Pancakes and a Birds Eye Potato Waffle with a curly smile of tomato sauce.

'Oh, I forgot the fork,' he says.

'S'OK,' I say, taking the plate.

'Why do you wanna sleep here?' he says.

'I like it better here,' I say.

The vestibule is freshly painted and feels fancy. Like my own private kingdom.

'You'll get cold,' he says. 'And you don't like spiders.'

'There won't be any spiders,' I say.

He knows I'll scream the house down at the sight of a daddy-long-legs.

Dad disappears again and comes back with one of his big old work jackets that he wears to the warehouse.

'OK, put this over you, then you won't get cold,' he says.

Now I am warm and snuggly.

I eat my tea and then I get sleepy.

Later, I wake up on the cold, hard floor. I can hear *Porridge* playing and Dad laughing loudly.

The next time I wake up I'm lying in my own bed.

November 2017

'Where would you say Carlisle is, George?'

I shift uncomfortably in my seat in the Memory Clinic.

'Where's Carlisle?' the woman repeats.

Dad does not answer.

I feel the pain of the silence acutely.

'Have you heard of it?'

He smiles. As if he's about to make a joke to cover up his shame. This is one of his tactics.

'Can you have a guess?' she says. He doesn't.

The woman marks something down in her notes.

I look her directly in the eye, hoping for some comeback. She looks away sharply.

Two weeks later we have it in print. A diagnosis. Dad has vascular dementia. There's no sense of relief. Just numbness.

January 2018

'I was in town before,' he says to me.

'Were you, Dad?' I say.

I am mashing a vast pan of Maris Pipers with butter and cream. There are sausages in the oven. I have frozen peas in the microwave, powdered gravy in a jug and a bag of Aunt Bessie's frozen Yorkshires on a baking sheet waiting to go.

If we all eat together then we are still a family. No matter what. Those are the rules, aren't they? How can it be the end if we're all still eating sausage and mash?

'And I saw this fella,' Dad rambles. 'He says, he says to me, "Oi, Scouse!" He says, "Hey, Scouse!" So I looked at him and it was … oh, I forget his name. Clive. Clive. Used to work with him. Helluvanice lad. Anyway. He had a little cat. A cat in a bag.'

My father is in a chatty mood. He has not left the house on his own for some months, although in his head he was in town just this morning.

All of us have our own tactics for dealing with my dad's confabulations; Mam tries to correct him when he talks, but this just makes him angry. He can't understand why she's undermining him and thinks she's doing it just to be awkward. Dave humours him. I try to draw the memory out. I like to squeeze it a bit further to see where it's going. I slip in questions about his daughters and his son when he's off his guard. But I cannot get any sense out of him. It feels a bit duplicitous. I've not popped back to London for weeks. My first *Guardian* columns have gone out to a largely positive reaction, but to get them done I've been leaning on Dave hard to keep an eye on things while I rush to Manchester and Birmingham. I have been writing from 5 a.m. until 2 p.m. and then trying to snatch naps while Dad and Mam have their afternoon snooze. Although I've learned the hard way about this; I opened my eyes last week to find that Dad had found my handbag, taken two sets of keys from the front pouch, unlocked the front door, then the porch door, and was behind the wheel of the Volvo, starting the engine. I cannot forgive myself. I keep imagining him in an overturned car on fire in a field or squashing kids on a zebra crossing.

'Grace, look at me, I'm on that hill,' Dad says, pointing out of the window.

'Oh yes, I see,' I say, stirring the gravy.

My tactic is to allow the fantasies, to just let them flow, as he looks happy. I like the communication. It's something, but even that is slipping away now. I know it can't last forever.

As sections of his brain furl up, he has trouble, when speaking, differentiating between thoughts and reality. If he looks out of the window up at the hill and his brain wants to make small talk about how cold it might be up there, he'll say, "Ere, Gracie, look at me blowing about on the hill. I am there, can you see me?'

'Ooh. Are you?' I say. 'Which one are you? You'll be tired when you get back, won't you?'

'Yes, I'll get blown off and land in the field.'

He laughs and walks off.

He is happy. And I'm happy to have communicated.

The problem with this tactic is that by the end of the day you are both as doolally as each other.

And every day of this madness is conducted in a haze of grief, but ambiguous grief, as you're bereaved of the person you love while babysitting their shell. Mam wonders if the diagnosis is an exaggeration. Maybe he needs a vitamin B12 injection? Maybe he is putting it on? We all agree he can't go into care.

May 2018

It is 1 a.m. and in a matter of hours I am supposed to be going to London on the 10.11 Penrith to Euston train to film *MasterChef* and then coming back via Leeds to review a restaurant, but Dad is in a small ball curled up on one side of his bed.

I think he is breathing.

I get very close.

He is breathing. He has not stood up for four days. I cannot get him to drink water. I take some bread with marmalade and a small square of chocolate, but I can't convince him to eat. Not even Dairy Milk Fruit & Nut. Is this what dying looks like? Or is he just tired? Or depressed? I look on the Internet to see if this is a stage of death. Me and Dave have not been able to wash him for weeks. He screams and shouts if we mention it. I think Dad is dying, but then he could possibly just be very dehydrated. How do you force someone to drink?

I look up bedsores. Rickets. Malnutrition.

I look up undertakers.

I look up Alzheimer's care homes. Outreach groups. The images are always of smiling people holding chinchillas from a local petting zoo. My father, I am quite sure, would rather be dead than do group activities.

Dad hates enforced fun. He never did a flippant thing or a hobby in his life. My father is ex-military, he is rough and wily, he does not do arts and crafts. I feel like I'm betraying him by even considering humiliating him in this way. Also, how would he act if he got there? He can be so cruel with his words.

But in the backgrounds of these pictures of dementia groups there are always people around me and my brother's age.

Relatives. Carers.

I want to hold my hand out and say, look, we are here too. Please help us. But I am too scared. Also, if we let other people into this situation, they could take events out of our hands.

I snap the laptop shut.

Dad is on his side in a ball. I check his breath with my hand in front of his face, then get into bed and wonder if he will last the night. At 6 a.m. he is still breathing. David tells me to go to London, so I set off for Penrith Station and hope Dad lasts until I get back.

June 2018

I cannot tell you about the weeks before my father stopped living with us.

Some of the things that he did. It was not him.

It was another person.

And I'll always feel that I let him down. I couldn't make him drink or eat, no matter what I cooked.

I knew under my watch he was going to die sooner than he should.

But the fact is that leaving him in his little room in the care home while he was crying, promising him I would definitely come back, has robbed me of a bit of my heart which will never grow back.

July 2018

Visiting Dad plays on my mind for at least seventy-two hours before I go. On trains, in hotel rooms and when I close my eyes to sleep. I must go. I must go. But it's a cloud over my day before I set off and I feel worse when it's done.

Dad is a skull in a chair.

Time, for him, is like a concertina. Opening and closing in the same sentence.

I sit in his little room. He sits on the side of his bed like an inmate.

Sometimes he cries. He cries for Mam, who he never sees – except Dave brought her to visit him yesterday, he just didn't recognise her.

He cries because I am keeping things from him.

He cries because he is a burden to me.

I like it best when he sleeps, as he is peaceful. I put on mid-afternoon reruns of *Emmerdale* and sit by the radiator in the room that no longer has a carpet – he cannot have carpet anymore, as he can't be trusted to tell anyone he needs the loo.

'Do you remember *A Touch of Frost*, Dad? Do you remember our Alsatian, Cilla?'

His mind is a snowstorm of fragments that partially happened and dreams and nightmares he firmly believes are true.

'Jesus is there in the roof tiles,' he says.

'The lads had all their sheepdogs out and I was referee.'

'There is a little cat in this room, Gracie, can you hear it?'

August 2018

In the main common room at the care home, a young woman from a local petting zoo has brought some live animals to show the residents.

A guinea pig.

A mouse.

A salamander.

'Everyone is in there,' says one of the ladies, beckoning me in.

I creep in at the back.

My dad is on the front row. Front and centre.

Almost everyone in the group has dementia.

I stand by the wall beside the weekly meals' menu, written in bright colours in Comic Sans.

Dad is engrossed in the guinea pig. He is soft and child-like, just like the people in the adverts I've seen for the dementia care groups. Like a little boy at nursery school.

He always loved animals.

The girl places the small bundle of fluff in his hands and he cuddles it to his chest, but he's clearly a little scared of it too.

August 2018

Mam and me are having a pot of tea and sultana scones together at 3 p.m. in a garden centre just outside Carlisle. It's the kind of simple thing we haven't been able to do for a very long time. For months leaving the house with Dad or without Dad was impossible.

I imagined things might be easier once we had moved him to the care home and he had nurses who could safely wash him and feed him and even boss him around a little without him screaming abuse. Also, his room has an alarm, so now he couldn't escape and get into the road or fall downstairs or set fire to anything.

But things are not easier, they are just differently hard.

Now Dad's gone, there's no wandering and no searching. He's no longer sleeping for so long that we have to go in and check he's breathing. There's no more worrying and putting off what will happen next. We just have much more time to think.

When we get back from the garden centre we sit in the lounge, me and Mam. Her treatment is ongoing, which means endless trips to the hospital for injections and pills. She is still stable but completely exhausted.

Day after day after day, we tell each other that we'll 'take it easy', but instead we end up fraught, conducting a laborious post-mortem of what has led us to this point.

It is all we can talk about.

It is the only thing to talk about.

Dad.

At least some of the stories are grimly funny. I remind her about the time I picked her up from hospital with him in tow, and in a blink between paying for the taxi and entering the building I lost him. Then, after some frantic searching, numerous elevator journeys and a tannoy call-out, I found him in the cafeteria running about pushing a wheelchair. It was very *Some Mothers Do 'Ave 'Em*.

'The daft bugger,' says Mam, laughing. 'We should have left him there then.'

I remind her about when he began to carry a leather flight bag around with him everywhere, even in the house, full of surreal items that he had decided were today's treasure. Me and Dave used to play a game called 'What is in the bag today?' One evening, after a particularly manic day, Dad fell asleep and we checked inside to find five neatly folded bobble hats.

'That bloody bag,' she laughs. 'He looked like Roy Cropper off *Corrie*. I put it in the bin one day and he fished it out.'

We talk about the beginning, years and years ago, when he started to leave the front door open, and then the car door standing wide open in supermarket car parks. And how he'd become lost on short shopping trips out and would then wait by the front door of the shop, furious that he had been abandoned.

We take all the pieces apart like a puzzle and put them back together over and over again. The accusations about a conspiracy, all the screaming and shouting and anger over imaginary events. How it all became less easy to be sympathetic about, and how eventually he was just plain frightening.

Mam is so tired. She has been chained to all of this for so many years. But now he has gone and she no longer wants to live freely. How can she just go out for a scone at a garden centre? Why should she live in freedom when we've put him in jail?

We talk and talk. Sometimes we get cross with each other and sit in separate rooms – me at her for not accepting this is what it is: this is us now. We could not get food, liquids or medication into him. We could not bathe him. He fell lots of times. Some very dangerous things happened when we were tired. We must try to move through this bit and see him being looked after properly as a positive. We can visit! Mam is frustrated at me for not saying that perhaps this is temporary.

'Maybe Dad will get better once he has had a rest too, and then we can get him home,' she says.

We argue, fall out and fall back in. I tell her I love her.

I try to make her laugh.

I remind her again about when he got hold of the car keys. This was not funny at all while it was happening. It could have been horrific.

I remind her of the months he pretended he was almost paraplegic and couldn't move his legs or arms, but when no one was looking he was fine, like the guy from *Little Britain*. That is actually pretty funny, on reflection.

Dad is no longer here, but he is still in every room we sit in for weeks and weeks and months and months. Dad's space at the table will always be empty. The wound I have about Dad only ever seems to grows the slenderest of scabs. The merest memory makes it bleed.

Things I miss about Dad

I miss when he ate the last roast potato at dinner and shouted, 'It's the fast and hungry in this house, Gracie.'

I miss when he described stupid folk by saying, 'He's about as much use as a one-legged man at an arse-kicking party.'

I miss him mispronouncing words to wind me up. Profiteroles as '*Profunferelos*', Yacht as '*yachet*'.

I miss him referring to my mother as '*Mein Führer*'.

I miss how he couldn't buy any item of clothing without it having a specific named purpose. 'I got these trousers for wearing to the lock-up,' he'd say. 'I got this jacket for walking the dog.' 'I got these pants for going for breakfast on the cruise.' If you wanted him to accept a new item, you had to sell its unique purpose. 'Happy Christmas, Dad! I got you these socks to put on if you're defrosting the car.'

I miss our shared black, twisted sense of humour. I once made him a sign in a medieval font that said, 'The Floggings will continue until Morale improves', which hung in the kitchen.

I miss him grassing me up to Mam to save his own skin during a silly family row, then jigging about in the background, mouthing, 'Your turn! Your turn! Your turn!'

I miss watching *Fawlty Towers* and Billy Connolly live on VHS.

I miss sending him Beryl Cook postcards of round-bottomed ladies in jacuzzis.

I miss listening to Johnny Cash albums in the car with him.

I miss him saying, 'Oh, leave her alone, she's only a little lass,' which he did even when I was forty.

I miss the WD-40, spare change, dust and random pieces of wood he left about the house.

I miss all these things and a million more.

'Does he still recognise you?' my friends ask when I explain why I'm no longer around.

'Sometimes,' I say. But I leave it there. I don't explain anything else.

Because in the moments when he recognises me, he is Dad. He's there. His facial muscles – very briefly – arrange themselves how they once did. But then he's gone again. It's over. And having him back for a few seconds just leaves me sore.

CHAPTER 11

Whelks in Jam

August 2018

Even with a head brimming with syrup and abject sadness, I need to go back out to work. I need the cash.

Maybe that is, after all, the true meaning of being working class.

For the last twenty-one days I have wandered around bra-less, in leggings, hollow-eyed and despondent, but this won't get the bills paid. It's impossible to review restaurants from under a duvet in a back bedroom in the remote Lake District.

So I'm back on the West Coast line from Penrith to Euston, stood in the toilet of Coach K. At Penrith I have red eyes from crying; by Oxenholme I have attached false eyelashes to my lids and let the glue dry, and swooshed myself thoroughly with a lint roller. As we pass through Lancaster, I have a packet of hair pins out and have the beginnings of an up-do. By Milton Keynes I am 60 per cent the person I once was, give or take the silver flecks in my hair that I hide clumsily with mascara. In a taxi at Euston Station I slip on a pair of heels, spray myself with Issey Miyake perfume and paint on a smile. Nothing is perfect, but I have definitely established a light veneer of London Me.

I'm off to review a totally ridiculous restaurant. It's not ridiculous in the eyes of the London food scene or the Michelin-star people, but it's certainly ridiculous if you've become accustomed to dining out in a garden centre.

This is a multi-million-pound-renovation West London dining experience. It involves a stark open kitchen where, as you arrive, a squadron of chefs are moving micro-fungi around plates intensely with silver tweezers. Many of the plates will be less like lunch, more like a Jenga game of shards and textures.

The restaurant's £50,000 Bose stereo system is playing *The Joshua Tree* by U2. The atmosphere when I arrive is tense. Really bloody tense. My attempt to book anonymously has clearly been thwarted. Most London restaurants use one of the same half-dozen reservation platforms these days, all leaving trails of electronic cookies wherever I leave my false names and phone numbers.

This has certainly happened here, as everyone from the door people to the chefs to the kitchen porter are being that kind of 'normal' where they bump into each other and smile with faces that look sore. Their hands wobble as they try to take a coat. Sometimes in these situations I see younger ones being taken aside and slapped down verbally for moving my glass too quickly, or too slowly, or not moving it at all. Sometimes waiters disappear in the middle of my dinner and

I cannot decide whether their shift has ended or they've been taken outside and executed. Sometimes I sit on the loo in newly built restaurants and hear the kitchen crews through the MDF wall being shouted at by chefs because my plate went out without garnish, which was the final straw in a terrible week, in a terrible year, for a chef who has not seen his wife or baby for weeks. In these cases, I'll act like I've not heard and one of the front-of-house staff will meet me outside the bathroom and escort me straight back to my seat to get me away from the noise. We will both discuss the recent weather and pretend everything is normal.

This is all normal.

It is normal that there's a picture of my face on the wall of every kitchen, with added notes on my likes and dislikes and more than likely with Satan's horns drawn on my forehead. On the days you're in the mood for all this, being a restaurant critic is an absolute blast. But the downside is that sometimes you're not and the cavalcade must go on. Off you must trot into another heavily staged room with freshly painted walls where everyone is smiling and oh so normal but also insane, to eat the very long tasting menu.

But first, as I reach the front desk, I must remember to put my shoulders back and tilt my chin semi-upwards and stick a swish in my step, just like my Aunt Frieda, and try to just ride the crackle of invisible chaos. The trick is to show them that here, exactly *here*, is where you're supposed to be.

The problem with this spanking new multi-million-pound restaurant is that it has absolutely zero buzz. Newly opened, millions frittered, big-name chefs, Michelin inspectors enraptured, previews in all the papers – but the word on the street is that it's as flat as a fluke. This is the cruellest of all scenarios. Everyone in the food scene respects you deeply, but the restaurant is bloody tedious and no one wants to hang out there.

The manager walks me over to a booth in the corner; a high-backed, deep-purple banquette worth the down payment on a small flat. It is the most comforting thing I have felt for a long while and I remember momentarily how tired and hungry I am, and that I am running on fumes. I'm haunted by Dad's face as we put him into the car to go to the care home, and tormented by how much I actually now miss him roaming the house, looking, always looking. I remind myself that by the time Dad went I had lost the ability to pacify him. I was just another face – sometimes his little girl, but sometimes just another gatekeeper to his peace. I was just the woman stopping him from finding that razor, in a drawer, behind the boots or at the bottom of his bag.

Matt appears, flanked by three front-of-house staff who are ensuring his path from the front door to the table is efficiently stage-managed and filled with effervescent small talk.

'Princess!' he cries. 'You look marvellous. A million dollars.'

True friends politely ignore the fact that you have aged at least ten years in six months and have begun cutting your own fringe with all-purpose kitchen scissors. That's proper friendship.

'Are you hungry?' I say, slightly mischievously.

'Very,' he says, unfurling his napkin.

This is a shame, because we're sitting down for a tasting menu that will not be a meal, but more a random collection of the chef's ambitions, presented with seventeen verses of Vogon poetry from the staff as they dole out tiny plates of his life story. These tomatoes remind chef of his grandmother's allotment. This eel is a tribute to his uncle's fishing prowess. I will pull the requisite faces to cope with all of this. The lunch will be purposefully challenging, at times confusing and served ritualistically in a manner that requires the diner to behave like a congregation member of a really obscure sect who knows specifically when to bow her head and when to pass the plate and what lines to utter when.

The menu is on a single sheet of paper. It doesn't feature names of dishes, but instead ingredients. For example: whelk, loganberry and whey.

These ingredients – either alone or in combination – won't even sound very delicious. They'll sound mysterious, puzzling and often downright off-putting.

If whelk is the first name on the list, it will almost definitely be course number one – unless the chef sends out three or four unadvertised courses beforehand, boosting the eight-course lunch up to twelve. I realise that nowadays almost all five-course tasting menus are actually around eight courses, because the chef will send 'palate cleansers' and 'amuse-bouches' and 'snacks' and 'extra courses'. This will seem generous but is actually just the restaurant buying time – a bit like when you go to a Beyoncé gig and three of the tracks are videos of her daughter at a family party, which is really cute, but it's just filler so Beyoncé can sit down and change her wig.

On being handed a menu like this, the acceptable reaction is to scan it with a sphinx-like gaze and say, 'Thank you, this looks wonderful.'

Secretly, you probably have some questions. Most normal human beings like to know what they're agreeing to eat and are dying to say, 'Whelk, loganberry and what? I mean, what even is that? What does it look like? Is it, like, the whelk in a jammy sauce? Or is it stewed berry with chopped whelk? And I don't even know what whey is in this context ... Will that be, like, milky or is it a powder?' For God's sake don't do this. The chef is a genius. This restaurant is his cerebral playground. Your role is not to reason why.

Being allergic to the whelk, however, is permittable. At that point the poor bastards in the kitchen will need to begin fumigating and scrubbing down surfaces and finding something even more ridiculous to swap it for.

A lamb's ear.

A carved artichoke.

A rare edible sedum cultivated in a Lancastrian polytunnel.

Fancy restaurants attract a lot of the sort of people who are convinced they'll bloat up into a spherical mass and then evaporate in a puff of pale-blue smoke if they were to so much as set eyes on a Weetabix. We begin our tasting-menu odyssey nibbling through plate after plate of grated bottarga, squid ink and aquilegia petals. We have one glass of wine, then another, then one more, then a sweet, sticky one just to celebrate being together.

On the train back to the Lakes I begin writing 700 words but find myself remembering a trip to London as a child in 1983. Me in a rainbow bomber jacket from the Littlewoods catalogue. Mam buying David and me bird seed in paper cartons to feed sparrows in our hands in St James's Park. Eating our first McDonald's on the Edgware Road; baulking at the gherkin and trying our first American-style root beer. Making Mam take me to Carnaby Street so I could find the *Smash Hits* office and pleading with her to let me wait for half an hour in a doorway while she and Dave went shopping so I could see the editor, Mark Ellen – the man responsible for amazing writers like Black Type – come out of the building to buy a coffee. I wanted to write and reach people and make them laugh like that. I put my forehead against the train window as it speeds through the Shap fells into the Lakes and try to take stock of the present. Regardless of the fog of ambiguous grief that makes every day twice as hard, I am now one of the most widely read restaurant critics on the planet; hundreds of thousands of people from all over the world visit my reviews weekly as I deliver small slices of joy or glorious schadenfreude. The reviews appear for free, pinged directly to their phones or their tablets, to be read on the loo, perhaps hiding from their children or even taking a breather from their own parent who has dementia. I think again of the little girl in the rainbow bomber jacket. She would be really chuffed.

November 2018

'We need to take some measurements,' she says.

The *Guardian Weekend* magazine's art team sound highly frazzled on the phone, as magazine folk always do when it's their job to make cover photoshoots happen quickly. It's late November and I have agreed, or at least not refused, to dress as a Christmas pudding on the front cover of the magazine, which we all agreed would be 'fun' three weeks ago but then swiftly forgot about, and now we have little time left to make a costume that fits me and try to shoot me in it, which isn't fun at all. And certainly not fun for the poor art-department person who now has the godawful task of calling a woman to find out the girth of her arse and boobs. The top section of the pudding is to be made of skin-tight white spandex to represent the brandy cream, with a white pelmet that will fall down from my waist over a brown puff-ball 'plum pudding' skirt.

'I don't know my measurements exactly,' I shout back, trying to cross the road outside Hamleys toy shop where a fake snow machine is in full gust and many stressed people who made less wise choices on contraception than myself are queueing with kids beside a live, dancing Santa's-little-helper display.

'OK, what dress size?' she asks gingerly.

I feel truly sorry for her having to ask. Dress sizes are shameful. She knows this, I know this.

'Dunno, ten, twelve, maybe? Or fourteen if it's made out of silk by a designer. What is the plum pudding bit made of?' I say, catching sight of myself in the Starbucks window on Regent Street and feeling short-changed by God yet again.

Why do I not get up earlier and run five miles a day?

Why have I started ordering *pommes aligot* again as a side on reviews?

Why have I lapsed and begun letting that delicious GAIL's Bakery olive bread into the house on weekends?

'You were size eight to ten on the cover shoot last year, Kanga – the stylist – says.'

I instantly feel worse.

I was good then.

I was better.

No, actually; I was slightly mentally ill with ambiguous grief, but my arms looked slim and amazing.

'I go up and down … top half thirty-four to thirty-six maybe? Depending on fabric. About a twenty-nine waist … Don't make anything skin-tight over my arse, for God's sake … Actually, hang on, can I call you back? I'm going into the BBC and I can't find my pass. Oh, I've got a call coming through from my brother, I'll have to take it.'

'He's gonna need all new clothes,' David says.

Dad has cut all of his clothes into narrow strips – all of them; all his underpants, all his trousers.

'What the fuck …? What did the nursing home say?'

'They say we're going to have to take away his scissors,' he says.

'How the hell did he get scissors?' I shout as I whisk along Regent Street. We both can't help laughing. It is awful but darkly hysterical. It feels good to hear each other's laughter again.

'I know – what else has he got, a set of nunchucks?' says my brother.

'I'm sorry, we've had to confiscate his shuriken throwing stars,' I say.

'We're sorry, he is no longer allowed his flamethrower.'

It feels amazing to laugh. Even if the world is burning.

'But why is he shredding his clothes?' I sigh as I walk into the BBC docs department and nod to Laurence and Georgia, my producers, and collect my script for a Radio 4 show about real-life dramas I've been working on called *The Untold*.

'Dunno, maybe he's going to a fancy-dress party as Robinson Crusoe,' my brother says. Sometimes Dave sounds exactly like Dad. Scouse tones lilt in his Cumbrian accent.

We both crack up laughing again. It is welcome. Cleansing.

And later, at midnight, I will remember that a Christmas pudding costume featuring a holly crown is being crafted using skew-whiff measurements for a size-ten-to-twelve woman, which I am almost definitely at this point not.

I'm the restaurant critic for the *Guardian* newspaper; I've eaten hundreds and hundreds of dinners, up and down the country this year alone.

The only tried and tested way to keep a steady weight in this job is to place sensitive electronic scales within two metres of my bed, stand on them every morning and then starve myself (sorry, fast – we call it fasting now) while power walking for several hours. And to continue this until the very next time you are contractually obliged by your newspaper to eat a six-course meal. I realise now that life is really too short to worry about these things.

Two days later, in the back of the studio in Islington, I'm squeezing and heaving into the Lycra brandy-butter top for the photoshoot, inwardly reminding myself that being a national newspaper restaurant critic is one of the greatest jobs in the world.

And I should never complain.

Not a word. I'm going to cling on tight and love every minute and be ready at any point to fight off all other contenders until gout finally carries me off.

The pudding outfit fits. Just. I breathe in as the stylist zips it up. We make space by hoisting my boobs up higher by tightening the bra straps. A stylist's trick, although you can end up with your nipples up by your tonsils.

We hide one of the trickier zips at the back by rearranging the nylon brandy-butter pelmet. I walk slowly in 180mm diamond heels to the set and the stylist gingerly hands me a prop to hold.

It is a three-feet-long 'match'. The biggest match in the world.

If Darlene Phillips from Brownies could find the box, she'd have a field day.

Now, as a plum pudding, I can pretend to set light to myself. I crack open one of the prop bottles of champagne with a pop and pour it into a coupe glass. This gets some quite solemn looks from the twenty-somethings on set who are rather straight-laced, but if you're going to spend the entire day looking like a berk with everyone staring at you, it pays to do it a little bit tipsy.

Also, I'm 45 – bloody ancient compared to them; my years of growing old atrociously have begun.

As the photographer shoots, I pose upright, brandishing my match, toasting the camera, holding a cute dog, swishing my skirt about, leaping in the air, drinking my champagne. Looking ecstatic. Looking pensive. Looking scared and confused by the match. Looking happy, looking knowing, looking crazy, looking smouldering – or more likely as though I have wind. As the camera snaps, a crowd of strangers stand around a laptop as the photos feed through onto the screen, saying nothing at all or sometimes yes, yes, no, that's good, no, these aren't working, are they?

And the photographer says, 'This is good, but less teeth – no, more eyes.' The best of these images are sent immediately through to the paper, who offer more feedback and begin laying out the front cover.

In December, the image of me as a human Christmas pudding is on the front page of the *Guardian Weekend*'s Christmas Food Special and also across the front of the main broadsheet paper. It is on newspaper stands and discussed on Sky News and beamed all over the world. I wish Dad could have seen it.

And I don't look too fat in the photos. Plus, at least the festive season means that the majority of restaurants close and there's no column to file for a fortnight.

I can use those days to peel off some pounds again.

Reset my clock.

Relearn how to feel hungry.

Cumbria, December 2018

Depression comes back like a bullet for Christmas. None of us can really be bothered with tinsel or carols in these circumstances, but we're all too polite to say it and try to make all the right sounds in front my niece, Lola, who is consumed by Snapchat so hopefully hasn't caught on. David says maybe we'll get a turkey tomorrow. Mam demands we take her to Workington ASDA to bulk-buy cut-price mince pies, but her brain is more ambitious than her body.

'I can walk! I'm fit enough to push a trolley,' she says. 'That woman with the sticky gun will be reducing all the good stuff and I'm missing it.' Ten minutes later she's asleep in a chair.

Feeling sheepish, I try to begin the gathering, the planning, the wrapping, then get back into bed and sleep too.

We'll begin … when we get time.

Maybe tomorrow?

Maybe we'll go out for Christmas lunch on the twenty-fifth? But no one makes a booking.

The fridge sits awkwardly empty right into the final week. By the 23rd of December the barren shelves feel downright weird. Tam puts up a small plastic tree with a few silver baubles. I shove a box of unwritten Christmas cards under the bed. I want the whole bloody season to just pass by and dump me in February. Watching cosy, jingly TV ads in every advert break feels like an act of self-harm.

At 2 p.m. on Christmas Eve, Dave and I look at each other and feel guilty.

We drive to the Penrith Sainsbury's.

'Give me one hour,' I say to him as he heads off to find last-minute gifts.

Something peculiar is sweeping over me. A feeling as old as time. I walk into the Christmas Eve chaos of a busy supermarket with a double-fronted trolley and begin. Almost on autopilot.

Parsnips
Spuds
Carrots
Cream – double, single, squirty
Butter
Cartons of custard
Brandy butter
A turkey
A nut roast
Sausage meat
Bread sauce

Whelks in Jam

Gravy powder
24 eggs
Hellman's mayo
Cranberry sauce
Pack of sausage rolls
Coleslaw
A ham
Trifle
Christmas pudding
Box of Paxo
Mint Matchmakers
Plastic tub of Quality Street
5 Mars selection boxes in a stocking shape
Bottle of Bacardi
Bottle of whisky
Bottle of Smirnoff
Bottle of Malibu
6 bottles of fizzy white
2 bottles of Liebfraumilch
6 bottles of red
12 cans of full-sugar Coca-Cola
5 types of cheese
Cream crackers
KP nuts
4 loaves of bread
24 white rolls
Big box of Christmas crackers
Heston Blumenthal croquembouche tower

Large full-butter stollen
24 star-topped mince pies
3 bags of satsumas
Smoked salmon
Crumpets
More bread
More packs of butter
A jar of mincemeat

I shop and shop, on and on, slightly demented, but high as a kite on the thrill of making the festive season happen, until the trolley is full to the brim and mince pies are falling out when I turn corners.

When we get home I begin to distribute the items around the house.

I have strategically vomited Christmas into every room and we are having it, whether everyone likes it or not.

I knock back a strong Bacardi and Coke, eat two Quality Street green triangles, lie down on the bed at 5 p.m. and fall asleep fully clothed, with my coat on.

Something has shifted.

Christmas Day, 2018

I'm standing in the kitchen in the bungalow in the Lakes drinking Cava and placing chipolata sausages wrapped in bacon onto a sheet pan, wearing felt antlers that jangle as I move. We had sourdough crumpets with smoked salmon for breakfast – very fancy, just like they do at Balmoral – and now Christmas dinner is going to happen. Mam is having one of her good days; she feels strong.

She's watching Jane McDonald's Christmas special and wowing at the glittery frocks as Jane croons through a festive special of contemporary classics in a red Hollywood-starlet number.

''Ere, you should have this show!' Mam says. 'You could do this.'

'I can't sing, Mam,' I say.

'You sang a lovely song once in a Bishop Goodwin assembly about a horse who lived in a lighthouse,' Mam says.

'I was seven, Mam,' I say.

'You're still seven to me,' she says, grabbing my hand. 'Well, more or less.'

Our entire home smells of turkey fat. Paul O'Grady is on Radio 2 chatting between Christmas classics. As the *poppa-poppa-poms* of Jona Lewie's 'Stop the Cavalry' begin, I feel my eyes fill up. I take a deep breath and distract myself with a box of Paxo. My iPhone beeps. It is a message from a lovely man I've been seeing called Charles. He has been at least one very good addition to my curious world.

Dave's car pulls in to the driveway outside the kitchen window.

He gets out and winks at me, then walks around to the passenger seat and leans in with his strong body-building arms. Then, carefully, he walks up the drive carrying a very small bundle of coats.

David is enormous; the body inside the coats is small and frail, but I can see its face laughing.

Mam appears beside me at the window, laughing.

'He's got him!' she shouts.

We all shout, 'Hello!'

Dave carries Dad gingerly through the house and plonks him down in the lounge in a big chair next to the telly.

Dad sits blinking, trying to get his bearings.

He is just a skull with a little bit of hair and a very thin body.

I crouch by his chair and say, 'Hello. Hello. It's Grace. It's Grace, Dad. Hello.'

He says, 'Oh! Throw. Throw. Throw.'

He splutters on his teeth, then stops, as if that made perfect sense.

I say, 'Yes!'

I know from the intonation that, if Dad had any of the words left, he'd be making a joke. My sister-in-law hands him a small glass of port. Dad uses my face on the front of the *Guardian Weekend* magazine as a coaster.

I say, 'How are you?'

He says, 'You here train? Train?'

I say, 'Yes, train.'

I sit down. We sit in silence, staring at each other.

I say, 'I love you, Dad. I love you.'

I hold his small, bony hand. He starts to cry.

I say, 'It's OK, Dad. Come on. No cry. Best dad. Best dad.'

He says, 'Sometimes I feel like – am – I am – *ppphhh*.'

I say, 'Shall we have a bit of chocolate?' I take the bar of Dairy Milk Fruit & Nut we got him for Christmas.

His eyes light up.

'My chocolate,' he says, and he pretends to take it off me.

We both laugh.

Epilogue

Grace Dent won the 2019 Guild of Food Writers Award for her essays on junk food and class. She continues to be the restaurant critic for the *Guardian* and appears regularly on the BBC television show *MasterChef*.

Mr Dent Snr's care home went into lockdown measures in March 2020, and he lived out the whole of the crisis in his favourite chair – which was viewable from the street – blissfully unaware that the pandemic existed. Very frail and mainly silent, George sleeps most of each day with a copy of the *Mirror* on his lap. His family can see him by appointment only. At some level, they reckon, he now has the life of which he always dreamed.

Mrs Dent Snr enjoyed *Hungry* but was keen to point out that it was yet more evidence of her daughter's overactive imagination. She also queried why her Franklin Mint Victorian figurine collection was not included in the home-decor passages. In late October 2020, Mrs Dent's cancer treatment began to fail. Grace Jr suspended work, headed north and moved into the spare room in her little flat. They spent their final ninety days together watching QVC, laughing, arguing and eating many slices of fruit cake. Mrs Dent died at home at 12.23 p.m. on 1 February 2021 with all her children present. She entered Carlisle Crematorium to the sound of 'Big Spender' by Shirley Bassey. She is missed desperately.

In July 2020, the UK Government banned advertising of junk food, both on TV and online, before 9 p.m., as well as Buy-One-Get-One free deals on high fat, salt and sugar products.

Acknowledgements

Thank you especially to Katya Shipster at HarperCollins for your patience and skill during this project and much gratitude to Dawn, Fionnuala, Jessie, Sarah, Holly, Julie, Anna, Tom, Alice, Ben, Ammara, Oli, Kate, Adam and Roger.

Thank you to Dylan for your eagle eye and help with the audiobook.

Thanks to Cathryn Summerhayes and Luke Speed at Curtis Brown, for their belief and enthusiasm.

Thank you, Charles, for your calmness and love.

Thank you, Tam, for everything you do.

Thank you to Matt, Tom and Courtney for your friendship.

And, of course, thank you, Mam and Dad, for everything.